Night-Scented Stock in Bloom?

Night-Scented Stock in Bloom?

Martha Robertson

The Pentland Press Limited
Edinburgh · Cambridge · Durham

© Martha Robertson 1993

First published in 1993 by
The Pentland Press Ltd.
1 Hutton Close
South Church
Bishop Auckland
Durham

All rights reserved.
Unauthorised duplication
contravenes existing laws.

ISBN 1 85821 035 6

Typeset by Elite Typesetting Techniques, Southampton.
Printed and bound by Antony Rowe Ltd., Chippenham.

To my niece, Patricia, for so willingly undertaking the typing of my manuscript to publishers' required standards

Contents

		Page
	Foreword	ix

Chapter

1.	Poetry – or Prose?	1
2.	Dialect Poetry	9
3.	Outward Bound	31
4.	The Place of Dialect Poetry in Literature	34
5.	Language	37
6.	Visions	42
7.	Vagaland and Housman	47
8.	The Catalyst	54
9.	'Gleanings From a Navvy's Scrapbook'	60
10.	The Welfare State	63
11.	The Pursuit of Knowledge	67
12.	Patriotism	69
13.	Religion	72
14.	Poetry and Religion	83
15.	The Mysterious World of Thought	93
16.	Civilization and Ethics	97
17.	Artificial Intelligence?	108
18.	The Mystery Beyond Investigation	112
19.	Island Magic	125
20.	The Seasons	137
21.	'The Star . . . Whose Worth's Unknown'	144

22.	'He Prayeth Best . . .'	150
23.	Eence Apon a Time . . .	159
24.	Viking Voyagers	165
25.	Disbelief Suspended!	171
26.	Lyric Poet	175
27.	The Sound of Music	189
28.	A Scottish Dialect?	195
29.	Guiding Us . . .	200

Foreword

After my husband's death in December 1973, I found, lying on a sidetable, the Weekly Review section of *The Sunday Times* (a paper which he had read regularly). It had a full-page article entitled 'Beyond our Understanding', sub-titled 'Arthur Koestler investigates the mysterious world of inexplicable coincidence'. The date of the newspaper was 25th November 1973, and I discover that I wrote at the top of the article: 'I found *The Sunday Times* open at this page after Alex's death. It was the last newspaper he was able to read. He died a month later, on 29th December 1973.'

That the 'supernatural' interested him I was well aware, but it was not a subject we discussed, nor, indeed, was my own interest very deep until, perhaps, during the year in which he died, when we both observed some unusual sequences of events and I began to make a note of them. I knew that my husband was not well, but as he had had indifferent health throughout our life together I was not accepting that this illness was to prove to be something beyond his normal stoical endurance. Looking back, the 'coincidences' here described seem in some strange way to have been influenced by my deep emotional stress following his illness and death, and continuing for a long time afterwards.

His poetry – mostly in the Shetland dialect – from my first reading of it, after we became engaged in 1952, seemed to proceed from perceptual gifts not available to more ordinary mortals. I remember that on reading those early manuscripts I was moved to tears, which psychiatry might possibly attribute to the fact that I was at that time on the verge of a very severe breakdown. But my own unaltered view is that I was given, through the poetry, an insight into the spiritual quality of the mind behind it. This conviction must have considerably strengthened by the time of my husband's death, for within a month or so I was engaged in editing *The Collected Poems of Vagaland*. 'Vagaland' was the name under which T. A. Robertson wrote.

The help and guidance given me, so often quite fortuitously, was such that I was never in doubt that the poetry was intended for a wider public. By November 1974, the work was in the hands of the printers, and it was from this time onwards that I developed a deep interest in reading, so much previously neglected, for various reasons, throughout a long lifetime! It was the 'coincidences' connected with my reading that astonished me most.

I think it was Arthur Koestler's theory that occurrences such as I shall describe are for some reason mostly observed by those undergoing emotional stress, creating conditions for reception of what would appear to be significant messages from the world of thought, which is there at all times for humanity to draw upon. Did not Teilhard de Chardin have a theory about the 'Noosphere'?

I make no apology for including in nearly every chapter selections from Vagaland's poetry. The poems have a way of linking themselves to whatever circumstance is under discussion, and, as the Orkney poet, Robert Rendall, aptly remarked when reviewing Vagaland's first book of poems, 'The local setting of such poetry . . . does not hinder it from having universal significance: the poems of the Greek Anthology are framed in the Aegean but mirror the world.'

Chapter 1

Poetry – or Prose?

In his *History of Scottish Literature* (1977) Maurice Lindsay quotes Scottish writer, Kenneth Buthlay, as saying: 'Surely we are right to protest against, or at least regret, the loss of those subtler qualities in the handling of language that used to make the poet's words so quotable.'

In my reading after my husband's death in 1973, I renewed acquaintance with these lines by Walter de la Mare:

> Look thy last on all things lovely
>   every hour. Let no night
> Seal thy sense in deathly slumber
>   till to delight
> Thou have paid thy utmost blessing,
>   Since that all things thou wouldst praise
> Beauty took from those that loved them
>   in other days.

The poem, easy to memorise, and thus 'so quotable', reminded me how much my own awareness of 'things to be praised' owed to friendship, but most of all to a securely happy married partnership. Furthermore, poetry of this kind which has a philosophy to convey, and which can be memorised, may provide a balm for aching hearts.

'*Poeta nascitur, non fit*' (the poet is born, not made) is surely as true today as when written about 2,000 years ago.

Included among my husband's papers I found a bookmark with the words 'Poetry is the music of the soul', and music indeed it should be, but, besides, you have to believe in the soul! So far as the music is concerned, its power is conveyed by Yeats:

> . . . When I was young
> I had not given a penny for a song
> Did not the poet sing it with such airs
> That one believed he had a sword upstairs.

The distinction between prose and poetry should, I think, be restored, although prose, too, can have the musical qualities which used to be required of poetry. In Chambers' *Biographical Dictionary* it is said of Nathaniel Hawthorne (the American novelist and short-story writer) that 'with little faculty for poetry, he had a singular command of the musical qualities of prose.' And it was Montaigne who wrote: 'The best prose is that which is most full of poetry.' But a line between prose and poetry was drawn by Alexander Pope:

> And he whose fustian's so sublimely bad
> It is not poetry, but prose run mad.
>
> (Epistle to Dr. Arbuthnot)

The following extract from Robert Lynd's Introduction to *An Anthology of Modern Verse* (1921) edited by Sir A. Methuen, puts the case for poetry in another way. (The anthology must have been a popular one, as it had by 1954 been reprinted thirty-nine times.)

> 'I had a little nut tree
>   Nothing would it bear
> But a silver nutmeg
>   And a golden pear.
> The King of Spain's daughter
>   Came to visit me
> And all because
>   Of my little nut tree.

'You might easily construct a theory of poetry, taking this most charming of nursery songs as your text. Here, better than in many a more pompous poem, you can see what it is that distinguishes poetry from prose. Here is the imagination escaping from the four walls – laughing at the four walls – and building its own house out of nothing but beauty and rhymes. Like all fine things it is a thing of pleasant sights and sounds – of images and music. Prose, too, can give us these delights. But verse which gives them to us is what we specifically call poetry.'

However, in his book *Enemies of Society* (1977), Paul Johnson writes:

'The verbal operation, so common in poetry, where the initial challenge enhances the depth of understanding eventually secured, is like the painter's art of chiaroscuro, where the density of shadows makes the highlights more brilliant.'

But should not both poetry and prose have a reasonable degree of intelligibility to as many minds as possible? Is there not sometimes a lack of courage to put the case direct? 'Tell the vision and write it plain,' wrote the prophet Habakkuk. One imagines that such poetry as has survived down the ages does not usually have to be searched for a meaning, although classical allusions – a stumbling block to those without a classical education – may present difficulty for the average reader.

It was the view of Richard Church that 'poetry, and, indeed, all art, should in its first purpose be a communication, as direct and simple as possible, while carrying the content of the artist's sincere purpose' ("Over the Bridge"). And it was Pascal who wrote: 'When we encounter a natural style we are always surprised and delighted, for we thought to see an author and found a man.' And Keats, in a letter to John Taylor in 1818, wrote, 'If poetry comes not as naturally as the leaves to a tree, it had better not come at all.'

In the last few decades books on every kind of topic have been flooding the market, including books and anthologies of present-day poetry. One imagines that at no period in Britain's history has so much encouragement been given to British writers, the British Arts Council standing in place of the wealthy patrons of art of olden days. How much of present-day poetry will survive into the next century is a matter for conjecture. One learns that neither Shelley nor Keats reached any wide reading public until a generation after their deaths.

Perhaps a fair comment on much recent poetry might be what is reputed to have been said by a college student to Robert Graves when Professor: 'A poem isn't something to be enjoyed: it's something to be analysed!'

These views about poetry will be considered by many to be old-fashioned. Even dictionary definitions of 'poetry' have changed remarkably in forty years or so. My copy of Chambers' *Twentieth-Century Dictionary* (a reprint in 1939) defines 'poetry' as, 'the art of expressing in melodious words the thoughts which are the creations of feeling and imagination: utterance in song: metrical composition.'

while the *Concise Oxford Dictionary* (1976) says 'poetry' is,

'art or work of the poet; elevated expression of elevated thought or feeling in metrical or rhythmical form; quality (in anything) that calls for poetic expression.'

And according to the latter dictionary it seems that what was once known as 'poetic prose' has now become 'prose poetry', defined as being 'prose having all the qualities of poetry except metre'. Here one is tempted to turn again to the assessment of Hawthorne's writing (in Chambers' *Biographical Dictionary*): 'With little faculty for poetry, Hawthorne had a singular command of the musical qualities of prose.'

The present era seems to be one of experimentation – not only in all the arts, but also in the sciences, and, one might add, most of all in moral values!

Of the two dictionary definitions of poetry quoted earlier, I still prefer the first! 'The elevated expression of elevated thought or feeling' would seem to emanate more from the intellect than the soul, in which latter I still believe! And, besides, there is the 'music of the soul' to be heard in such lines as:

> Softly along the road of evening
> In a twilight dim with rose,
> Wrinkled with age, and drenched with dew
> Old Nod, the shepherd, goes.

(Walter de la Mare)

These memorable lines were quoted to me by my husband in his last illness at a time when sleep was eluding him.

There has been a revival in the poetry of Kipling, Robert Service and many others. Indeed the variety of poetry now being published seems to be aimed at a much wider reading public than could have been reached a few decades back. One would hope that the long-established poets may find their way back into the curricula of schools and colleges. Good poetry is a legacy to be enjoyed by young and old, and if memorised in youth can be a source of strength and pleasure, to be drawn on throughout life.

But, if I heard aright, during an interview some years ago in the radio programme *Bookshelf*, a representative of the Arts Council for Great Britain indicated that we should no longer be asking 'Does this man rhyme, does this man scan?' This may mean the Oxford Dictionary definition of poetry having to be revised still further. Unless poetry retains something of its original quality of memorableness, it will be available to fewer and fewer people.

Compare this situation with that which has provided us down the centuries with a legacy of epic poems, ballads, nursery rhymes, etc. One thinks of the Norn 'Hildina Ballad', one of the very rare examples of Norn language surviving in Shetland in 1774. The remnants of this ballad were preserved simply because it could still be recited by a very old man to an interested visitor in the lonely island of Foula. In the same way, much of Shetland dialect poetry, with its still surviving remnants of Norn, will be preserved through the enthusiasm of children, who, encouraged by parents and teachers, show a remarkable aptitude for memorising even the longest poems. 'I have cared but little for the poetry I cannot memorise' are the words of Birrell, biographer of W. P. Ker.

English poetry in the past has been recognized as falling into certain categories. There have been the 'classical' poets, the 'metaphysical' poets, the 'romantic' poets, and so on. I am not aware that a name has yet been given to the present age of poetry. Judging from the following note in Maurice Lindsay's *History of Scottish Literature* (p. 14), it seems that my husband's poetry, of which more later, may fall partly into the 'romantic' category, dealing largely as it does with historical and folk material:

> 'Romance enmeshes historical and folk material which has no correspondence in ancient literature. Romance laid the foundation of modern prose fiction, its passion for story-telling never having been assuaged. It eventually gave rise to the conception of Romanticism, encouraging energy, fancy and freedom as opposed to the lucidity and order of Classicism.'

And yet there is so much 'lucidity and order' in the poetry of my husband (*Vagaland*) that it must also contain much Classicism!

Swinburne, according to Chambers' *Biographical Dictionary*, represented 'the last phase of the Romantic movement – with a little posthumous life in the early Yeats.'

Night-Scented Stock in Bloom?

This may be the place to recount a remarkable personal experience – more than coincidence, surely? – involving the poetry of Swinburne.

For many months after my husband's death my time was wholly devoted to the editing of his collected poems, and radio listening was restricted to news broadcasts. One afternoon, when my reading of proofs was completed and the book was in the hands of the printers, I delayed switching off the radio after listening to the news, and in an hour or so found myself listening to a play – involuntarily, at first, because for some time previously the type of play being broadcast had not appealed to either myself or my husband! This one proved to be something different, however, its sensitivity and poetic tones riveting my attention and leaving me deeply affected. I am not ashamed to confess that I am a highly emotional person and had been undergoing great emotional stress.

Convinced that the play meant something special for me – why should I have been so convinced? – I hurried to my sister's house next door to consult her *Radio Times* as to the name of the play and its author. (I had neither purchased nor read a *Radio Times* for almost a year.)

I found that the play had been written by R. C. Scriven, an author then not known to me, and that its title was *And a Measure of Sliding Sand* – a very unusual name for a play, I thought. Also mentioned in the *Radio Times* was a book called *The Seasons of the Blind*, by the same author. It could be purchased from the B.B.C. I decided to order it.

Two days later I was present at a talk given by the minister of our church, in which he mentioned, in passing, the poet Swinburne, indicating that the latter's view of life, to judge from his writing, had been that of an atheist. Remembering this remark next day, I decided to look in our *Golden Treasury* for poems by Swinburne. I found six, read through each one with interest, and, in the second verse of the last poem[1], came on the words 'And a measure of sliding sand'! I literally gasped with astonishment.

To understand the full significance, for me, of this experience, it has to be remembered that, as explained elsewhere, I had never up to this point in my life been an avid reader.

When *The Seasons of the Blind*, a book of five plays by R. C. Scriven, arrived from the B.B.C., further coincidences occurred which will not all be mentioned, but from introductory remarks to the plays I did learn that A. E. Housman had been one of the playwright's favourite poets. My

---

[1] *Atalanta in Calydon* – Shepherd's Chorus.

husband throughout his life was a devotee of Housman's poetry, and before our marriage had explored the Shropshire countryside and places associated with the poet and his 'Shropshire Lad'.

I made a further discovery. Stage instructions for the plays were that some of the work of Delius should be played as background music. Now, my husband always claimed that he was tone deaf – this may seem remarkable in a poet – yet, when we had listened (in the late 1960s?) to a television programme called *A Song of Summer* (based on the life of Delius) my husband kept saying to me, 'Pat, I like that music.' It was only when reading the plays by R. C. Scriven that I realised that a poem 'Simmer Sang', one of the last written by my husband, owed its title to the music of Delius.

Opinion is divided as to what may have been the nature of Swinburne's religious belief. Alfred Noyes, in his autobiography *Two Worlds for Memory* tells of Swinburne that one of his favourite lines was:

We are what suns and winds and waters make us

but certainly the lines he wrote on the death of his father, Admiral Swinburne, are clearly the response of an agnostic rather than an atheist:

Whose sail went seaward yesterday from shore
   To cross the last of many an unknown sea.
The life, the spirit and the work were one
   That here – ah, who shall say, that here are done?
Not I, that know not; father, not thy son,
   For all the darkness of the night and sea.

Alfred Noyes concluded: 'This was the real Swinburne, the Swinburne who, as I saw him at The Pines, impressed me with the essential nobility of his mind and spirit.'

A conviction of the significance of so many of my experiences, noted down over a long period of years, has led me to introduce them, not only in association with my husband's poetry but also in association with the expression of strongly held personal views on present-day controversial topics. This has resulted in a somewhat unusual format of writing.

I can only deduce that the forces which have impelled me to write have been directed simply and solely by the mysterious bond of love which is recognized by many to be 'stronger than death'. The views I have tried to express are put forward in good faith and as a mere lay person's small contribution towards reappraisal of ethical values when dealing with the baffling problems which arise in modern science and technology.

Chapter 2

Dialect poetry

In writing now about dialect, and dialect poetry in particular, I hope not to lose the interest of anyone who has stayed with me thus far! My husband, a true scholar, well read in languages classical and modern, and with a particular facility for English which he taught in school, was nevertheless an adamant defender of his native dialect, which he called 'Shetlanrie' when giving a title to the following poem – a humorous answer to a letter sent to our local paper by an ex-islander living in New Zealand, who had been absent from his homeland for fifty years. (For impatient readers a translation follows the dialect poem.)

> Some dösna laek wir dialect and dis is what dey say:
> 'We ocht to dö awa wi it – hit's truly hed its day,
> An hit's no wirt a boddie's while ta spaek it; onywye,
> Hit's brokken English, brokken Scots, and idder bruk firbye.'
>
> Dis view I dönna favour, an der wan thing very clear,
> We're hed dis Shetlan dialect fir twartree hunder year;
> An if you geng ta study it, A'm shöre at you'll agree
> Der Norn wirds atil it, jöst as plain as dey can be.
>
> Noo, if a boat you mention, dan der mony a Norn name
> Fae da tilfers ida boddim, ta da stamreen at da stem.
> An hit's Norn wirds you're spaekin whin you wirk ita da hill
> Wi da tushkar at you cast wi and da kishie at you fill.

An you couldna dö withoot dem whin you're scrapin möldie-bletts
Or aandooin fir piltiks roond da baas an at da kletts;
Ya, da Norn still is wi wis, and hit's waddered mony a baff –
We öse it still apo da laand an fram apo da haaf.

Der little doot da dialect haes loks o English wirds
An if you look fir Scots eens, dan you fin dem dere in mirds.
An I winder wha could tell me if der onything at's wrang
Wi wirds at Scott wret mony a time and Robbie Burns sang.

An as fir 'brokken English', dey wid laekly less be said
Aboot it if dey tocht what wye da English speech wis med.
What is dis English, onywye? Dey took da wirds dey fan
In Latin, Greek, and idder tungs, an altered every wan.

Der naethin wrang wi dat, you kyin, what sood dey idder dö?
Bit if dey altered Latin we can alter English tö.
Da English is a aacht ta hae whin you're awa fae haem;
You hae ta meet wi uncan folk an you maan spaek wi dem.

Bit here ita da Isles hit's laek a pair o Sunday shön,
Ower weel ta pit apo you whin your daily wark is döne;
Dey're no what you'd be wearin ta geng buksin trowe a mire,
Or rowin oot apo da voe, or kyerryin fae da byre.

Sae ony een at wants can k-nap as muckle as dey laek,
Bit lat wis keep da Shetlan wirds at we're bön wint ta spaek.
Dey're maybe no perskeet, you kyin, dey're maybe haemaboot,
Bit what we're aalwis hed we widna laek ta dö withoot!

A Translation of 'Shetlanrie'

Some folks don't like our dialect and this is what they say:
'We ought to do away with it – it's truly had its day.
And it's not worth while to speak it; anyhow
It's broken English, broken Scots and other rubbish too.'
This view I do not favour, and there's one thing very clear –
We've had this Shetland dialect for two or three hundred years;
And if you come to study it, I'm sure that you'll agree
There are Norn words in it, just as plain as they can be.

Now, if a boat you mention, then there's many a Norn name
From the 'Tilfers' (loose floor boards) in the bottom, to the 'stamreen' (knee-timber) at the stem.
And it's Norn words you're speaking when you work out on the (peat) hill,
With the 'tushkar' (peat cutter) that you cast (cut peats with) and the 'kishie' (straw basket) that you fill.

And you couldn't do without them when you're scraping 'möldie-bletts' (areas of peat mould)
Or 'aandooin' (rowing slowly) for 'piltiks' (coalfish)
    round the 'baas' (sunken rocks) and at the 'kletts' (earthfast rocks near shore).
Yes, the Norn still is with us, and it's weathered many a 'baff' (struggle)
We use it still upon the land and 'fram apo da haaf' (far out at sea).

There's little doubt the dialect has lots of English words,
And if you look for Scots ones you'll find 'dem dere in mirds' (plenty of them too).
And I wonder who could tell me if there's anything that's wrong
With words that Scott wrote many a time, and Robbie Burns sang.

And as for broken English, there would likely less be said,
About it if they thought about the way the English speech was made.
What is this English anyway? They took the words they 'fan' (found)
In Latin, Greek and other tongues, and altered every 'wan' (one).

There's nothing wrong with that, you know, what else should they do?
But if they altered Latin we can alter English too.
English is a possession worth having when you're far away from 'haem' (home)
You have to meet with 'uncan folk' (strangers) and you must speak with them.

But English here in the isles is like a pair of Sunday 'shön' (shoes)
All right for putting on when your daily work is done;
They're not what you'd be wearing to go 'buksin' (walking heavily) through a mire,
Or rowing out upon the 'voe' (inlet of the sea) or 'carrying from the byre'

So anyone who wants (to) can 'k-nap' (speak in an affected way) as much as they like,
But let us keep the Shetland words that we've been accustomed to.
They're maybe not 'perskeet' (fastidious) you know, they're maybe 'haemaboot' (rather homely),
But what we've always had we wouldn't like to be 'withoot'!

The story of how the dialect came into existence is rather complex. The Shetland Islands belonged to Denmark and Norway over 500 years ago, and Norn was the language then spoken by the islanders. In 1462 the King of Denmark and Norway gave the islands 'in pledge' to Scotland, as a dowry for his daughter, Princess Margaret, who was to marry the Scottish King. It was a strange contract, and, possibly because in those times, and in succeeding centuries, the distant islands had little significance for the Danish crown then holding sway over Scandinavia, the 'pledge' was never redeemed.

Although Norn had been the language of Shetland for more than 700 years, no Norn literature has survived in the islands except what little was handed down orally, and one can only conjecture what may have happened. It is my own theory that such literature as existed would have been in the possession of the then ruling classes in these islands – the Danes and/or Norwegians – and it seems reasonable to suppose that they, rather than remain under alien rule, went back to Scandinavia, taking their personal possessions, including any writings, with them.[1] Then there is the fact that incomers from Scotland, and later from England, who settled in the islands from the sixteenth century onwards, could not understand the Norn language and its use was more and more discouraged. But the native Norn speech must have persisted for a long time, for, as mentioned earlier, the original Norn ballads were still being recited in the remote island of Foula in 1774, more than 300 years after the transfer of the islands.

In Shetland's traditional 'Unst Boat Song', with its remnants of Norn, the word 'Obadea' occurs repeatedly. Formerly, this, when being translated, was thought to be possibly the equivalent of the Norwegian word 'obyde' (meaning 'hurt, trouble or annoyance'). However, another inter-

---

[1] This view is sustained by Hibbert in his *Shetland Islands* (1822) where he writes concerning the rule of the Scottish Earl Patrick Stewart: 'During this dominion of terror, wealthy Scandinavians are reported to have hastily sold to Scottish inhabitants their estates and interests in the country, seeking a refuge in the more kindly bosom of the parent region.'

pretation, given more recently by a Norwegian friend, is that there is a reference here to the Obadiah (pronounced in Norn 'Obadea'?) prophecy in the Catholic Bible concerning the abandonment of a whole people to foreign rule. The islands 'pawned' by King Christian I of Denmark were, as explained above, never redeemed.

It may be of interest to add that Norway herself under the Danish crown had 400 years of 'national non-existence' until achieving independence in 1814, and during this period her literature, including the writings of the new Church after the Reformation, seems to have been written mostly in Danish, the language of the capital, Copenhagen. So it is hardly to be wondered at that Shetland from 1462 onwards gradually lost any possible heritage of original Norn writings.

Times must indeed have been hard for the islanders. The new settlers, who over the centuries acquired much of their land, did not understand their language, and, for the most part, it seems, did not attempt to, with the result that Norn as a language in its own right gradually became diluted with Middle Scots, and later Middle English, until we have the dialect as it exists today.

One must, however, give credit to those among incoming Scots and English who did their utmost to introduce education to the islands, though in doing so they unfeelingly discouraged the use of Norn, or any adaptation of it. To this day one hears of a schoolmaster who would not allow the dialect to be spoken even in the playground! Suppression of their native language must have felt by these schoolchildren like being 'pulled up by the roots'. Even had the Education Act (1870) been introduced some two or three centuries earlier, while Norn was still a living language, one wonders whether the islanders would have been allowed to become bilingual, in the sense of being able to read and write in two distinct languages. I recall reading as a child at our primary school an English translation of *La Dernière Classe* by Alphonse Daudet, a deeply moving account, though I did not then realise that a very similar imposition had been made on the Norn language of the Shetlanders. Elsewhere I have explained that I myself am of purely Scottish mainland descent!

The first school in Shetland was in the village of Waas[2] (which appears as 'Walls' on ordnance maps – a clear mistranslation from the Norn). The *Hjaltland Miscellany*, Volume II, compiled and edited in 1937 by Christina Jamieson and E. S. Reid Tait, tells us that, 'In 1768 the Minister, Session, Heritors and Inhabitants of Walls rose and built themselves a

---

[2] In 1713. Waas, in Norn, means 'voes' or 'inlets of the sea'.

school, which was for fifty years the principal school in the islands .... It had the proud distinction of being the only school in which Latin was taught. Its site, and the land attached to it, were gifted to the Parish by Mr. Buchan (the then minister) and it is known as 'Happyhansel' to this day.' This was the school which my husband-to-be and myself were to attend more than a century and a half later. It is noteworthy that it was built 100 years before the Education Act of 1870, when education became compulsory throughout the United Kingdom.

At first sight it may seem that the Shetland dialect is ungrammatical, but this is not so. It would be truer, I think, to say that it has preserved its links with the past and is a living language which has not had in any way to be revived, as was found necessary in the case of Lallans, for instance, the language of the Lowland Scots. Links with the speech of early English and Scots settlers are readily seen in the Shetland dialect. For example, the word 'catched' used in seventeenth century English literature is still to be heard in present day Shetland speech. The use of the singular form of the verb after a plural noun is a legacy from Middle Scots, and a number of words such as 'Joolie' (July) retain their Middle Scots or Middle English pronunciation.

'Der', meaning 'there is' or 'there are', is simply two Norwegian words *'det er'* which have been telescoped. Spelling becomes a problem when dealing with the future tense, e.g. 'Dey'll be' (Nor. *'det vil'*) means 'there will be', because 'dey' is the nearest equivalent in sound to the Norwegian *'det'*.

Grammatical errors do tend to creep in when mistaken attempts are made to convert these Norn words into English. For instance, I have heard 'der', when meaning 'there are', converted into *'they* are' – what a betrayal of a genuine Norn heritage! The catch here, of course, is that, generally speaking, the English 'th' is sounded 'd' in the Shetland dialect. For example, 'the' (Eng.), 'da' (Shetland).

A defence of the dialect, dictated to me by my husband shortly before his death, was published posthumously in *The New Shetlander* in the Spring number 1974. The oil era was already with us. What its full effects would be were not yet known, but it was obvious that the traditional life and language of the islands might be threatened. The message, unedited by me in any way, which he left for his fellow Shetlanders was this:

'The tractor has replaced the spade, and outboard motors are now more commonly seen than "kabes"[3] and "humlibaands".[3] In

---

[3] Kabe – pin in gunwale of boat, i.e. oar-rest; humlibaand – loop through which oar is passed.

some places people have resorted to oil-fired central heating instead of relying on the "tushkar"[4] to supply them with fuel.

'The Shetland dialect, however, is still with us. It remains the everyday speech of the great majority of older Shetlanders and the younger generation have not yet abandoned it, although life in the islands is very different now from what it was before the advent of radio and television. In days gone by many Shetland children seldom heard English spoken until they went to school. Now transistor radios and TV sets bring it to them in their infancy.

'Some years ago the Education Committee, among their further education classes, sponsored a Shetland studies class, and it is a great pity that this was discontinued, as it brought together people with different views about dialect, all of which proved to be extremely interesting. What emerged from the discussions was general agreement about the chances which the dialect had of surviving. As far as I can remember, it was the view of all who attended the class that people who came into Shetland hardly ever objected to their children learning the dialect. I know for a fact that this was the case in Waas where I went to school. Out of a roll of about seventy pupils almost a quarter were incomers. One or two, who were senior pupils when they began to attend the school, spoke English. Of those who started school about the age of five, all, as far as I can recollect, learned to speak the dialect.

'The headmaster of the school and his assistant teacher were not Shetlanders, and everyone inside the walls of the school's two classrooms spoke English. Once outside the school door, however, almost everyone, including three of the headmaster's sons who were at school in my time, spoke nothing but Shetland dialect.

'The members of the Shetland Studies group agreed that one serious threat to the dialect was the attitude of some Shetland parents, who wanted their children to "get on" and, thinking the dialect was an impediment to progress, adopted a policy of encouraging their offspring to 'spaek proper'.

'It seems that there have always been some people in Shetland with a feeling of inferiority about their own speech, regarding it,

---

[4] Tushkar – peat cutter.

at best, as something that should be spoken only if it is not meant to be taken seriously. A number of writers, some of them native-born Shetlanders, have referred to Shetland words in a disparaging way as "corruptions" of English words, or of Norse words. This is an attitude which I find it impossible to comprehend. Apparently it was quite all right for the inhabitants of England to change the Latin name "Londinium" to "London", but the Shetlanders who changed the name "Hundsvord" to "Hunsfirt" are accused of having "corrupted" an old Norse name. The people of Shetland, apparently, should not have constructed a dialect out of Norn, Scots and English by altering the words of these languages, but the people of England after the Norman Conquest were quite at liberty to form a language by modifying words from West Saxon, Danish and Norman-French, to which, as time went by, there were added versions of words from Latin, Greek, and almost every other language under the sun. No one, so far as I know, says that the English word "orchard" is a "corruption" of Old English "ort-geard", or that "window" is a "corruption" of "vindauga". These words, we are told, are "derived" from Anglo-Saxon and Icelandic. If this is so, why should the expressive dialect word "moaniment" be considered a corruption of English "monument", instead of a derivative from it?[5]

'Whether it is a good thing or not for languages to change greatly is quite another question. The people of Iceland, and Gaelic speakers in Scotland, seem to have got along without making very many changes in their ancient form of speech. The point is that speakers of modern English are the last people in the world in a position to criticise others for altering words. One has only to open an etymological dictionary of the English language to find that the words in it are practically all alterations and modifications of other words.

'In connection with this, it is interesting to note that there are quite a number of words in the Shetland dialect which have changed less than their counterparts in English. For example, the

---

[5] I have discovered that 'moniment' is the last word of Spenser's Epithalamion written in the sixteenth century! It derives from the Latin 'monimentum' so that, in form, our Shetland word 'moaniment' is nearer the original after all! Also I find that Ben Jonson's poem to the memory of William Shakespeare has the line 'Thou art a moniment . . .!' (the word here being used, of course, in its original sense whereas in present-day Shetland dialect the word has come to mean a 'stupid' or 'foolish person'). M.R.

word "holiday" was originally a "holy day" and that is how it is still pronounced in the dialect. In a game of cards, the Shetland "trumph" is closer to the original than English "trump", for a "trump card" was, to begin with, a "triumph card". The seventeenth-century poet, Sir John Suckling, in his poem "A Ballad upon a Wedding", made "newly" rhyme with "July". This does not mean that his rhyming was faulty. It means that he pronounced the name of the month "Joolie" as those who keep to the old dialect still pronounce it in Shetland.

'These words, and others which are still closely connected with an older form of English, only exemplify one of the many interesting things about Shetland dialect. The great work compiled by Dr. Jakob Jakobsen only covers a part of the dialect, that part which comes from the Norn language once spoken in the Islands. Glossaries and word-lists have been produced by Arthur Edmondston, James Stout Angus and others. Much more information about dialect words and expressions could still be obtained by intensive study of the local forms of dialect spoken in different parts of Shetland.[6]

'There is no need for anyone who writes down Shetland dialect to insert a superfluity of apostrophes. This practice suggests that the dialect is merely mispronounced English. In fact, our dialect was mainly based on two languages, the Shetland Norn, which died out some time after Shetland had become part of Scotland, and the old Scots tongue, which ceased to be a national language after England and Scotland were united. It is worth noting that more people in Scotland are now becoming aware of their linguistic heritage. Sir David Lindsay's play, *The Thrie Estaites*, written in sixteenth-century Scots, which was presented in the Assembly Hall in Edinburgh, has been described as one of the highlights of the 1973 Edinburgh Festival.

'The grammatical structure of the old Scots language became the main part of the foundation of the Shetland dialect, which replaced Norn, as had formerly been spoken, by the middle of the eighteenth century. But Norn was not completely swept away by the flood of new words and expressions which the Shetland

---

[6] As recently as December 1979 a *Dictionary of Dialect Words and Expressions* in use in central Shetland has been compiled by John J. Graham (published by The Thule Press). Revised Edition 1984 (published by The Shetland Publishing Company). M.R.

people learned. Thousands of old words, and many phrases and idioms which still survive in the dialect, can be traced back to the Norn tongue.

'What must be admitted is that our Shetland speech is not a language. In fact, it is not a single dialect but rather a group of dialects, and no one of these has any special status. In other words, while one form of English is accepted as standard English, there is no standard Shetland dialect. Because of this, Shetland dialect, unlike English, could not, at the present time, be taught as a separate language. It could, however, be a subject of study, and Shetland school children in top primary and secondary classes should be encouraged to study it, as well as the few remnants of the Norn language which were eventually written down.

'I remember on one occasion hearing Mr. George Mowat, then headmaster of Moray House Demonstration School in Edinburgh, and also an authority on teaching method, stating that 'a knowledge of dialect leads to flexibility of mind', and others who have studied the subject have been of the same opinion.

'A monoglot speaker has nothing with which to compare words which he hears being used, and there is a possibility that he may accept and use them without really considering what they mean. A great many words which we find in newspapers and books, or hear nowadays on radio or television, are either vague, ambiguous, or, in some cases, have no meaning at all. For example "democracy" is one example of a word that has completely lost any meaning that it originally had. It can now be applied to a country with a government freely elected by the people or to a state controlled by a dictator. When you listen to the radio or watch television you hear people continually using words such as "relationship" or "immaturity" to put forward a point of view, or prove a case, and interviewers and studio audiences apparently accept these words without questioning their meaning. A knowledge of a dialect, or of another language, enables a person to examine words, compare them with words or phrases which would be used in the other language or in a down-to-earth dialect, and decide if they have any real meaning or are really only part of a web of expressions which could trap anyone who accepts them without thinking about them. This in itself is one good reason for retaining our Shetland speech.

'Furthermore, although there is no unified Shetland dialect, there is no reason why the people of Shetland should not have one, if they want it. Some of the Norwegian people, who did not approve of the Dano-Norwegian language, which was the official language of their country when it was closely linked with Denmark, constructed a language of their own (Nynorsk) out of words and phrases taken from the different dialects of Norway, and they avoided the danger of creating an artificial language by consulting dialect speakers all over the country, making sure that every word and every phrase would be used in a natural, not a made-up way. The result is that they now have a language of their own, in addition to the local dialects which are still spoken.

'In Shetland, a great many words have been collected, not only by writers and folklorists, past and present, but also by a number of people who have been contributing information to Dr. David Murison, editor of *The Scottish National Dictionary*, who has recorded Shetland dialect words, along with dialect words from all parts of Scotland. What is required now in Shetland is a really comprehensive collection of the idiomatic phrases and expressions which are the life-blood of Shetland dialect.

'Given such a collection, in addition to Jakobsen's *Dictionary* and the various lists and glossaries of words which were not recorded by him it should be possible for an interested group of people from different parts of Shetland to construct a generally accepted form of dialect which would not replace local forms of dialect, but could be used by Shetland writers, as Nynorsk is used in Norway.

'The reason why the Norn language died was that not even a small number of the Shetland people were sufficiently interested in preserving it. If our present-day speech is not to suffer the same fate, something similar to what has been done in Norway will have to be undertaken without more delay in Shetland.

'It may be said that Norway is a nation, while Shetland is a small island community. For an example of what can be done by people in a community we may look at what has happened in Cornwall. Cornish died out as a spoken language about the year 1800, but groups of enthusiasts revived it from existing dialect words, place names, and what had been, fortunately for them, written down in their old language.

'In 1967 the Cornish Language Board was formed and the policy of this body seems to me to be a wonderful example to people in all minority groups who are interested in retaining their own kind of speech.

'An article on the Cornish Language Board appeared in the Gaelic-English periodical *Sruth* in 1968. I have to thank Mr. P. A. S. Pool, Secretary of the Board, who wrote the article, for permission to quote from it. In the first place Mr. Pool says: "It has been decided that the Board shall have no connection with any political organisation, the revival of the language being regarded as a matter of culture rather than politics." Referring to the aims of the Cornish Language Board, he goes on to say: "The main object of the Board is to make Cornish readily available as an optional second language for those Cornish people who want it, to offer them back a vital part of their heritage of which they were deprived centuries ago by apathy and a series of historical accidents. We have no wish to see Cornish replace English as the first language of Cornish people, and none to make its learning or use compulsory at any time or for any purpose. Although it is one of our cherished hopes to see the language taught in Cornish schools and available as a subject in public examinations, we realise that this must be purely on an optional basis. The Board will never seek to force Cornish on school children or anyone else. . . . ."

'This, in my opinion, should also be the aim of people who are still attached to the old Shetland dialect. I have no doubt that there are at the present time many people in Shetland who have the same feelings about their own speech as the writer of the article about the Cornish language had about his when he wrote: ". . . in an age when so much of Cornwall's future seems dark, the Cornish people may yet find that the revival of their language revives also their pride in being Cornish."[7]

'In conclusion, therefore, I would like to pass on to the people of Shetland a statement about our own dialect, which, it is related, was made on an occasion when an old Shetlander, whom Dr. Jacobsen was consulting about Shetland words, remarked that some people did not like the Shetland dialect. "You have a beautiful dialect," replied Dr. Jacobsen. "Those who do not like it do not understand it."'

---

[7] An interesting news item on Radio 4 (U.K), on 19th September 1979, was that for the first time in 200 years the Cornish language had been used in a baptismal service. It was anticipated that the child baptised would grow up familiar with, and able to speak, his native language. M.R.

Dialect Poetry

And the beauty of the dialect was probably never better illustrated than by Vagaland himself who used its rhythms and tones to such effect, as in his poem 'Kwarna Farna?'[8] described by one critic as a 'miniature of genius':

> A laar o Wast wind blaain
> keeps doon da waarm ön;
> I hear da baas o Huxter,
> an hear da laverik's tön
> ita da lift abön.
>
> Da lochs, trowe bricht daals lyin,
> spreads wide dir sheenin net;
> da simmermil is mirrlin
> by skerry, stack and klett;
> bit shön da sun will set.
>
> You see noo every saison
> run waas o barns an byres,
> an riggs an cuts fast shangin
> ta burra an ta mires,
> an little reek fae fires.
>
> Eence Dale ta Brouster mustered
> a thoosand folk an mair
> ta dell, an draa da boats doon,
> an cast, an maa, an shair;
> bit noo da laand is bare.

The poem 'Kwarna Farna?' with its sad reference to depopulation, first appeared in *The New Shetlander* in 1947. It was a time of economic depression, more and more crofts lying neglected, the menfolk, who had been through the war, being still in the Merchant Navy, and, thanks to

---

[8] 'Kwarna Farna?' Where are you going?

---

laar – light breeze; ön – air; baas – sunken rocks with sea breaking on them; laverik – lark; tön – tune; lift – sky; daals – valleys; simmermil – shimmer on water; mirrlin – vibrating; skerry – rock, away from mainland; stack – high rock; klett – earth-fast rock on seashore; run waas – fallen walls; riggs – cultivated fields; cuts – cultivated strips separated by ditches; burra – heath rush; eence – at one time, formerly; dell – dig; cast – cut peats; maa – mow; shair – cut corn with a sickle; Dale ta Brouster – within this area was the village of Waas.

sheep subsidies, land once cultivated having been given over to sheep raising. I remember my horror, on returning to Shetland in 1952 (after an absence of twenty years) on finding the manse glebe given over wholly to sheep. In World War I, at another period when menfolk were away in the services, my mother had organised the cultivation of that land to its fullest possible extent, assisted by her husband and three small daughters (we had been aged only ten, eight and six years, respectively, when the 1914 war broke out!). Help was given freely, of course, by neighbour families, especially in 'Voar' (Spring) and 'Hairst' (harvest).[9] An account of the agricultural activities and achievements of my mother would fill another book! It is not an exaggeration to say that all was achieved in those days by 'toil and sweat'. That a living was wrested from the soil by bare hands and the simplest of tools is indicated by the last verse of 'Kwarna Farna?'

And in another poem, 'Da Aald Magic', Vagaland recalls memories of life as it was lived in our young days:

> I saa da water glansin bricht
>   apo da voe as we göd roond
> Rowin oot by ta Tunisdale
>   or sailin trowe da Aester Soond.
>
> I felt agyin da kishie-baand
>   aroond my shooders grippen ticht;
> A kishie-foo o hard, blue paets
>   apo your back is no ower licht.
>
> I saa da lasses at da roog,
>   fillin da flittin-kishies dere,
> Da men an laads gyaain ower da geng
>   ta lodd da flittie at da ayre –
>
> An aa da wark at we wid dö
>   (an we hed mony a tirin day);
> I saa da time whin we were young,
>   da fun at we wir wint ta hae.

---

[9] I learn that 'Voar' and 'Hairst' are words also existing in Faeroese and Icelandic.

---

göd – went; Aester Soond – East Sound (of Waas); kishie – peat basket; shooders – shoulders; roog – heap (here, of peats); flitting-kishies – baskets used when peats were transported by sea; geng – wooden plank; flittie – boat for transporting peats; ayre – shore, beach; wark – work; wid – would; wir – were; wint – wont.

Dialect Poetry

In one of the reviews of *The Collected Poems* published in 1975, Vagaland was described as 'a poet of the countryside like Wordsworth and Clare'. 'Hjalta' is a poem which, I imagine, speaks to the hearts of all Shetlanders who love their native landscape, giving expression as it does to feelings often difficult to put into words:

> Da eart-bark in among da girse
> Is glintin whaar you stride,
> An antrin seggie lowin up
> Closs be da burn side.
> Da blugga, laek da golden sun,
> Is blazin far an wide.
>
> You see da lukkaminnie's oo
> In hentins spread an drift;
> An da mey-flooer cleds da burn-broo
> An growes ita da clift.
> Da kokkilurie covers aa
> Laek da white cloods ower da lift.
>
> Der places oot alang da loch
> At yöle-girse sweetly fills;
> An smora lukks da drummie-bee
> Wi da waff at da lang swaar spills;
> Da hedder-ön is da very braeth
> O da Sooth wind ower da hills.
>
> You dönna see da Simmer pass,
> Rose-red wi laamer een;
> You see a glöd o blue an gold,
> A glisk o white an green;
> Onlie da Sooth wind sees an seichs
> Ta tink at shö is geen.

---

eart-bark – tormentil; girse – grass; antrin – occasional; seggie – wild iris; lowin – (literally) flaming; blugga – marsh marigold; lukkaminnie's oo – cotton sedge; hentins – tufts; mey-flooer – primrose; broo – bank; clift – cleft, cliff; kokkilurie – daisy; lift – sky; yöle-girse – meadowsweet; smora – clover; lukks – entices; drummie-bee – bumble-bee; waff – waft; swaar – swath; hedder-ön – scent of heather; laamer – amber; glöd – glow; glisk – gleam; onlie (pronounced onnlie) – only; seichs – sighs.

Ernest Marwick, who wrote the introduction to *The Collected Poems*, quoted the third verse of 'Hjalta' to illustrate how 'T. A. Robertson could evoke the landscape of Shetland so intensely that the nostrils twitched with its remembered fragrance.'

'Smora' is the Shetland word for clover. It grows freely in places on the supposed lawn around this house, and I may say that I delight in the scent of it when mowing the grass!

The word 'hentins' refers to the tufts and scraps of wool which drift on to fences and over the hillsides when sheep are ready for 'rooin'. This indicates how easily the wool can be stripped from Shetland sheep.[10] The word 'hentins', however, had a special meaning for me after this experience, noted down on 19th May 1977:

'At our local theatre last night a film slide show was presented to raise funds for Christian Aid. There were readings and songs to illustrate the message of the films. Larry and Shirley Peterson were there, and their songs included "Hae ye ony moorit oo?". The words are by Vagaland, the music by Larry. On radio this morning, in the children's religious service, the bible story of Ruth was told, and how she gleaned the corn left by the harvesters. For the first time I saw a direct analogy with the collecting of 'hentins' in Shetland's days of deprivation.'

The poem 'Hae ye ony moorit oo?' was appropriately used on this occasion for it had been written by Vagaland for World Refugee Year. His concern for those in want was genuine, for he had first-hand experience in childhood and youth of occasions when living standards were reduced to the barest necessities. Here is the poem:

'Boy,' aald graand-daa said ta me,
'I sall tell a story,
Aa aboot da days at's geen,
An folk at lived afore dee.

---

[10]And also, it seems, from English sheep in the sixteenth century, as we learn from these two lines in Christopher Marlowe's poem 'The Passionate Shepherd to His Love':

A gown made of the finest wooll
Which from our pretty lambs we pull . . .

'Eence a poor cam ta wir crö,
　　Shö wis caald an fantin;
Dis wis aa at shö wid say,
　　Whin aksed what shö wis wantin:

'"Hae ye ony moorit oo,
　　An hae ye ony mair o 'it?
Hae ye ony beni-pluckins
　　At I could get a hair o 'it?"

'Dat wis what shö wantit, folk,
　　Ta keep da life atil her –
A grain o oo ta caird an spin
　　An mak an sell fir siller.'

Yun wis graand-daa's tell, ye see,
　　What folk hed ta siffer –
Da story o da human race,
　　Hit never seems ta differ.

Hit's little better nooadays,
　　Pain an black fantation,
Haemless, wanless refugees,
　　Fae every hattered nation.

Hae ye ony siller, folk,
　　An hae ye ony mair o 'it?
Ye'll mind aboot da refugees
　　fir dey wid need a share o 'it.

　An early dialect poem, 'Wir Midder-Tung' (adapted from the Danish of Edvard Lembcke) reveals the depth of the poet's feeling for his native speech:

---

poor(n) – poor, helpless person; crö – enclosure for sheep; fantin – hungry; moorit oo – light brown wool; beni-pluckins – inferior wool; grain – small quantity; tell – tale; fantation – famine; wanless – friendless, forlorn; hattered – oppressed.

Night-Scented Stock in Bloom?

Wir Midder-Tung is boannie; hit haes a haemly vynd;
What wye am I ta röse hit? Hit pits ita my mind
    A maiden sae fair, a bride at's shön ta be,
    An shö is sae young an sae fainly fir ta see.

Da fremmd folk wis tinkin dey widna lat her spaek;
Dey traetened her wi traldim athin her ain toon-daek;
    Bit jöst whin dey tocht dey wid binnd her, fit an haand
    Shö gae sic a gaff at shö brook da strongest baand.

Shö gae her skalds da pooer ta spaek wi wirds o micht;
An noo dey staand aroond her, sae nane ta her can licht.
    Da sangs at we sing an da stories at we tell,
    Dey're link-stens apon her röf ta hadd him fae da gael.

Wir names apo da Fitstöl, wi dadderie an steer,
Will shön be forgotten, laek da snaa o fern-year;
    An folk will aye faad —Time will never lat dem be —
    Bit shö is aye young an sae boannie fir ta see.

but even more eloquent are these lines from another early poem:

>Trowe wir minds wir ain aald language
>   still keeps rinnin laek a tön;
>Laek da laverik ida hömin,
>   sheerlin whin da day is döne;
>Laek da seich o wind trowe coarn
>   at da risin o da mön.

Widely appreciated though this poetry has been throughout the islands, and by ex-islanders in different parts of the world, it has still, I think, to find its true place in the field of Scottish national poetry. Despite the dialect's strong links with Middle Scots as well as Old Norn, where

---

haemly vynd – pleasant, homely way (of expressing itself); ta röse – praise; fainly – comely; fremmd folk – strangers; traetened – threatened; traldim – slavery; toon-daek – boundary of township; gaff – loud laugh; brook – broke; skalds – poets; licht ta – beset; link-stens – stones, with ropes attached to keep a roof from being torn by the wind; röf – roof; hadd – hold fast; gael – gale; Fitstöl – the Earth; dadderie an steer – drudgery and exertion; shön – soon; fern-year – last year; faad – fade; tön – tune; laverik – skylark; hömin – twilight; sheerlin – singing; seich – sigh.

literature is concerned Shetland is not willingly accepted as part of Scotland. Indeed, in *A History of Scottish Literature* (1974), Orkney and Shetland are referred to dismissively as the 'Norse islands'. I have not heard them thus designated where the oil industry is concerned!

It is only fair, however, to quote from a review by George Campbell Hay in *The Scotsman* of 11th September 1965: 'After all, Shetland is Scottish and Scots must have the breadth of mind to live with Norn as they live with Gaelic, Scots and English.'

A book entitled *Grammar and Usage of the Shetland Dialect*, compiled in 1952[11] by T. A. Robertson and John Graham, says in its Introduction:

'From about the fifteenth century onwards Scots began to influence the spoken language. The following examples from fifteenth-century Scottish poetry show the historical origin of our current usage in the present indicative of verbs:

"For wyffis sayis that lukand werk is lycht."

"Na thing of lufe I knaw,
But keipis my scheip under yone wid."

"And burnis hurlis all their bankis doune."

'While the influence of modern English is obviously making itself felt on the dialect, earlier English influences are also apparent, such as some striking affinities with seventeenth-century literature. In *The Pilgrim's Progress*, for example, we find that the word 'habitation' is used for 'house', and the past tense of 'catch' is 'catched', as in

"Here he espied his roll; the which he, with
trembling and haste, catched up. . ."

'The reflexive verb is frequently used, as in:

"Thither, therefore, Christian got, where also
he sat down to rest him."

---

[11] reprinted by *The Shetland Times* in September 1991.

'We wish to refute the argument that certain forms of Shetland dialect are 'broken English'. John Bunyan, one of the greatest figures in literature, did not write "broken English".'

I entered in my notebook, on 7th January 1977, a curious coincidence in connection with the writing of John Bunyan. Our speaker in church the previous Sunday had said how much he liked the Shetland word 'lichtsim', meaning 'cheery', 'pleasant', 'happy'. A few days later I read in *The Pilgrim's Progress*: 'Then was Christian glad and *lightsome*.'

In my reading it has been interesting to discover how many dialect words inherited from Middle English and Middle Scots retain their original pronunciation. For example, in Surrey's sixteenth-century poem 'On the Death of Sir Thomas Wyatt' the word 'gost' (ghost) is found to rhyme with 'lost' in the next line. It is still pronounced thus in Shetland.

Again, in these two lines from 'Answer to the Third Epistle' by Allan Ramsay (1686–1758):

> That bang'ster billy Caesar July
> Wha at Pharsalia wan the tooly.[12]

'July' (here, of course, standing for Julius) is obviously pronounced 'Joolie' as in Shetland to this day when referring to the month of July.

And there are numerous other examples of dialect words which preserve their Middle Scots origins, e.g.:

Middle Scots	Shetland
'scho' (she)	'shö'
'brocken' (broken)	'brokken'
'sclait' (slate)	'sklate'
'thackit' (thatched)	'tekkit'
	etc.

The word 'tooly' in the foregoing quotation from Allan Ramsay's poem is interesting as regards both pronunciation and meaning. Compare its use as a verb in Vagaland's poem 'Gennem Aarene' (a translation from the Danish of Poul Pedersen):

---

[12] Tooly – battle.

Da far cloods sail trowe lang days
at nane can hadd or binnd,
As Voar wi Winter tölies
ta da nönin o da wind.

In his book *Literature and Gentility in Scotland* David Daiches mentions that King James VI of Scotland wrote an 'Admonition to the Master poet to be waar of great bragging'. A highly humorous song composed some fifty years ago by a local composer, Ally Linklater, has this line:

Ir you been waar o ony trows? (trolls)

'waar' being the old form of 'aware'.

There is little doubt that the dialect's evolution from Middle English and Middle Scots (in combination, of course, with Old Norn) could be a subject for separate research as regards word form, grammar and pronunciation. In the meantime, the point could, I think, with justice be made that in Shetland an element of *Scottish* literature evolved naturally, and undisturbed, for the most part, by the influences following the Unions of 1603 and 1707 indicated by David Daiches in *Literature and Gentility in Scotland*.

Anyone studying the Shetland dialect will have noticed how the English relative pronoun 'that' is represented by 'at' in Shetland speech, e.g. 'Da Sangs at A'll Sing ta Dee'. A closely related form of this relative pronoun is found in the following old Scottish motto which was quoted by Jane Oliver in *The Blue Heaven Bends over All*:

'He yt tholis overcomis'
(He that endures overcomes)

However, when used as a demonstrative pronoun, an adjective, or an adverb, 'that' in English becomes 'dat' in Shetland dialect. There is thus a strict grammatical distinction between 'at' and 'dat'.

From the few examples quoted it will be seen that the Shetland dialect has in fact preserved a good deal of the old Scots tongue from which present day Scottish speech has evolved! On the other hand, the Norn influence is still everywhere apparent in such words as 'dukki' (doll - cf.

---

tölies – battles, struggles; nönin – sighing sound.

Ibsen's 'Et Dukkihjem'); 'caavie' (snowstorm - cf. Nor. 'snø-kave'); 'mareel' (phosphorescence) - cf. Nor. 'moreld'; etc. And many words and phrases are vividly expressive, e.g. 'döless' (indolent); 'vyndless' (clumsy); 'trang' (busy); 'pellet' (ragged), e.g. a 'pellet röl' (used of a pony); 'filskit' (light-hearted, almost 'flippant'); 'hatter' (affliction). The number is endless. Phrases like 'wi dat sam', meaning 'immediately afterwards', have their exact counterpart in Norwegian, cf. 'med det samme'. And what could be more expressive than 'apo da aidge o a time' (meaning 'very rarely'), or more concise than 'ere da streen' (the night before last, 'da streen' meaning 'last night').

Vagaland, in his article about the Shetland dialect, drew a parallel with attempts being made to preserve the Cornish language. The parallel extends also to the Gaelic and Welsh languages. Concerning the last-mentioned, Peter Simple wrote in *The Scotsman* of 12th July 1979: 'Without some knowledge of that which underlies our past – are not the Welsh the heirs of Roman Britain? – we can understand neither our history nor ourselves.'

Boswell, in his *Journal of a Tour to the Hebrides*, makes a similar observation: 'There is no tracing the connection of ancient nations but by language; and therefore I am always sorry when any language is lost, because languages are the pedigree of nations.'

Chapter 3

Outward Bound

On behalf of the Shetland Folk Society, of which he was secretary for twenty-seven years, Vagaland in his last year edited a book of Shetland Songs, entitled *Da Sangs at A'll Sing ta Dee*, which he lived to see published in November 1973.

Almost in the same week another book, from the same publishers (The Shetland Times of Lerwick), appeared. This was *New Shetlander Writing*, an anthology selected from the first 100 numbers of *The New Shetlander*, edited by John and Laurence Graham. To this periodical, which first appeared shortly after the end of World War Two, Vagaland had contributed regularly, and, indeed, it was in this publication that his poetry first appeared. During his illness I had had little opportunity to look at the anthology, but I recall that after his death I stood in a dazed condition by the table on which the book lay, idly turning a few pages, when suddenly the following poem by him caught my attention:

Alamootie

'They frequent the smaller islands as a rule, yet you may have a picnic on one of these islands within a few feet of a hundred alamooties and never see one of them, nor indeed have the slightest indication that such creatures are in existence.' – G.T.K.

    Da sea comes in by Fugla Skerry
    Fae da Western Ocean's fardest brink
    An froads aroond green holms an islands
    Aa patterned ower wi da banks-flooers' pink.
    It's dere at you fin da alamooties,

Night-Scented Stock in Bloom?

If you kyin ta look fir a quiet place
Trowe da rabbit-hols, an stens, an bluster
Ida islands whaar dey nest in paece.

Da peerie fools is lyin waarm
An little dey kyin o da wirld ootside –
Da livin green o da eart abön dem,
Da blue o da lift, an da waters wide,
Whaar da midder-bird, trowe sun or stimna,
Sets oot at da first o da moarnin licht
An only comes ashore ta maet dem
Wi da dim starn-sheen or da mönless nicht.

Dere dey lie trowe da days o Simmer
Dere dey bide till da Hairst comes in,
An dey're left ta face da storms o Winter
Wi no a hirnik o da kin.
Wi nane ta tell dem whaar dey're gyaain
Or what dey'll see on dir first strange vaige
Dey lift dir flicht ower da Western Ocean
An dey mak fir da far haaf's ootmist aidge.

Sae wi man – he lives a saison
Apo da aidge o a boondless sea,
A peerie life in a peerie wirld
An aa benon is a mystery.
Bit it's no ida eart at he'll be lyin
Whin ta da end o his life he's wun,
Fir da sowl gengs fram laek da alamootie
As da lift growes bricht wi da moarnin sun.

Mention of *The New Shetlander* recalls that a copy of this magazine chanced to meet the eye of one of the residents of an American state prison about forty years ago. It appears that he was a writer, and in a letter to the then editor of *The New Shetlander* he gave the following touching

---

alamootie – storm petrel; banks – flooer – sea-pink; bluster – kind of peat with fibrous roots in it; fools – birds (Nor. fugl); lift – sky; stimna – thick mist; maet – feed; starn-sheen – starlight; no a hirnik o da kin – not a single relative (parent, here?); vaige – voyage; far haaf – outer ocean; ootmist aidge – far horizon; benon – beyond; fram – forth.

Outward Bound

assessment of a Vagaland poem which he had just read: 'I have gone to your poetry for a start, because the songs are the way to hear any tongue, I think. I don't know how highly you rate "Firelicht" by Vagaland, but it couldn't be any higher than I do. This has . . . tremendous appeal to me. It is a beautiful thing.'

Here is the poem 'Firelicht':

> Da sun flings doon his golden licht
>   Sae veeve apo da voe;
> Da mön shö sheens laek siller bricht
>   Ower da hills an daals below;
> Bit da licht at lukks a boddie haem
>   Ower da langest, weariest gaets
> Is da licht at's apon his ain hert-sten
>   Fae a fire o lowin paets.
>
> You geng ta mony a uncan place,
>   An you meet blyde-spaekin folk;
> You look at mony a freendly face
>   Awa fae your ain Aald Rock
> Bit da haem-wind blaas, an you böst ta vaige
>   Back ower da lang sea-rodds
> An your ain folk's wylcom waarms your hert
>   Laek da haet o da göd blue clods.
>
> Sae we'll sing a sang o da hard blue clods,
>   An we'll röse da black paet-banks;
> Da mossy skyumpiks an bluster tö,
>   Fir dem we'll gie wir tanks.
> Der maybe things at we dönna hae
>   At you finn in idder laands,
> Bit da boanniest sicht ida wirld ta see
>   Is da lichtsome glöd fae da taands.

---

veeve – vivid; lukks – entices; gaets – paths; hert-sten – hearthstone; lowin – burning brightly; uncan – strange; blyde-spaekin – pleasantly spoken; Da Aald Rock – (beloved) Shetland; böst ta – must; vaige – travel; blue clods – small hard peats; röse – praise; skyumpiks – big mossy peat; bluster – fibrous peat; der – there are; glöd – glow; taands – bright embers.

Chapter 4

The Place of Dialect Poetry in Literature

It is, perhaps, not generally known that on his father's side Vagaland (T. A. Robertson) was of Scottish descent, his antecedents, as members of the Robertson clan (Clan Donnachaidh), being understood to have fought at Culloden and escaped northwards. Because of the old custom through many generations, of giving patronymic surnames in Shetland, the tracing of ancestry is no easy matter, but relatives in England and America are still pursuing lines of inquiry. In *Scotland's Magazine*, April 1966, A. D. Mackie wrote: 'the language in which Robertson writes is a mixture of standard Scots and Norn. The Scots in it is, in fact, closely akin to the dialect of Perthshire.' Perthshire is Clan Donnachaidh country.

Of recent years it has seemed to me a strange coincidence that the only mountain I have ever climbed – I am no mountaineer, having always been somewhat nervous of heights – is Schiehallion in Perthshire. I think it was in 1935 that the English friend with whom I was holidaying at Kinfauns Castle (at that time a Co-operative Holiday Association centre) persuaded me to join in this mountaineering expedition, and it was largely with her encouragement that I completed the ascent. This event took place long before my unforeseeable marriage in 1953. While the Robertson clan are recorded in history as supporters of the royal Stuarts, it also happens that descent from a branch of the Stuarts is claimed on my mother's side of our family!

I have often felt that Vagaland's lyrical gift was to a great extent Scottish. Much of it had something of the quality of the historical ballads of which he was so fond. At least a dozen different local composers have been inspired to make songs of some twenty of his lyrics, and it is hoped that these may one day be published as a collection.

Two small books of his poetry were published in his lifetime. His collected poems were published by The Shetland Times in 1975 and a paperback reprint was issued in 1980. All these books are now out of print.

The place of dialect poetry in literature is described by Kenneth Hopkins in *A Short History of English Poetry*. After discussing the work of some minor poets of the nineteenth century, he continues:

> 'At the same time a large literature of dialect poetry began to accumulate, some the work of cultured men like William Barnes and T. E. Brown, with occasional excursions into this field by the greater professional poets also. . . . The interest and value of this work will continue to increase as the process of everybody speaking a standard and colourless English accent goes on; and it preserves many vivid words and expressions, and records many local customs and eccentricities, which else would be entirely lost.'

There is, of course, renewed interest in Barnes, and a selection of his poems has been edited by Robert Nye, who says in his Introduction:

> 'It is impertinent to praise or dismiss him as a 'Dorset' poet, a poet whose relevance and achievement are local; and, besides, when that is done the task of assessing his peculiar use of language has hardly been touched. By dubbing that usage 'dialect' in fact, it is possible to ignore the issue of just how good this poet is.'

That last sentence could almost have been written about Shetland's poet, Vagaland.

Barnes's own preface to the 1862 collection of his poems reads:

> 'To write in what some may deem a fast out-wearing speech-form may seem as idle as the writing one's name in the snow of a spring day. I cannot help it. It is my mother tongue, and is to my mind the only true speech of the life that I draw.'

Vagaland wrote in similar vein:

Wir Midder-tung is boannie, hit haes a haemly vynd..

Rupert Brooke, who according to John Lehmann might have become one of the leading critics of his day, said this about poetry: 'It has been the repeated endeavour of half the great English poets to bring the language of poetry, and the accent and rhythm of poetry, nearer to the intensest moments of common speech.' (*Rupert Brooke – His Life and Legend*, by John Lehmann.)

In his Introduction to *The Collected Poems of Vagaland*, Ernest Marwick wrote:

> 'The fact that so many poems are in dialect should not prove an insuperable obstacle to their enjoyment by people who are unfamiliar with the Shetland tongue. Both the general sense and the poetic quality of most of the poems are easy to perceive. . . . Indeed, it seems to me that this book may fulfil a secondary function as a wholly delightful introduction to Shetland speech, never used with greater precision by any Shetland writer.'

It was reassuring to hear the opinion expressed on radio, by the editor of the Oxford Dictionary, that 'dialects have their own grammar'. The Shetland dialect has, indeed, its own definite grammatical forms, a fact to which attention was drawn as far back as 1952 by the joint editors of *Grammar and Usage of the Shetland Dialect*.

In the same radio 'phone-in' programme, it was also stressed that 'people should be bilingual', a point also made by T. A. Robertson (Vagaland) in his defence of the Shetland dialect (*New Shetlander* – Spring 1974).

Finally, it is surely significant that Thomas Hardy is reported to have regretted that, as a young man, on the advice of critics, he had cut out dialect words from his early poems, though they had no exact synonym to fit the context.

Chapter 5

Language

'Remember that you are a human being with a soul, and the divine gift of articulate speech . . .'
(Professor Higgins in *Pygmalion*, by Bernard Shaw)

Radio 'phone-in' programmes, letters to newspapers, periodicals, etc., all bear witness to concern about the rapid changes overtaking the English language. Probably not since the Norman Conquest, when the language of the invaders seems to have crossed and blended with the language of the conquered, have the changes been so observable in the span of a single generation. 'Shakespeare's pure English', as it was described by Auberon Waugh in *Books and Bookmen*, was standard reading in my own schooldays seventy years ago, and its perfection was then unchallenged and beyond criticism. Passages from the plays were memorised by schoolchildren – often under duress! but the beauty of the words and the wisdom they contained concerning every conceivable human experience were there to be recalled and drawn upon in later life. The standard of English written by Shakespeare in the sixteenth century was still supreme in the estimation of English scholars 300 years later, and was, and still is, held in high esteem by people of many nations other than our own.

The first function of language being to communicate, it is important that thoughts be expressed in clear and unequivocal words. Despite continuing efforts to banish Latin and Greek from our schools' curricula, and despite the contention in some fields of linguistics that the grammar of language should no longer be studied on a classical basis, the fact remains that a full understanding of the English language cannot be achieved without some acquaintance with its classical origins. In my own case, lack of any knowledge of Greek has hampered my understanding of the meaning of many words derived from that language.

It is clear that a language such as English, so frequently used in worldwide communication, should be used with precision to avoid misinterpretations and misunderstandings. It was recently aptly remarked on radio that we live in a modern Babel, where words are used to conceal meaning rather than to make it plain.

The proposition 'to' is now used almost indiscriminately after the verb 'compare', not only in the spoken, but often in the written word. I have always understood that when Shakespeare wrote 'Shall I compare thee to a summer's day?' he meant 'Shall I liken thee to a summer's day?' and that this was a somewhat exceptional use of the preposition 'to' after the verb 'compare'.

The *Concise Oxford Dictionary* makes this distinction between the prepositions 'to' and 'with' when used with the verb 'compare':

> To compare: to estimate similarity or dissimilarity (of one thing *to* another in quality, of one thing *with* another in quantity or detailed nature)

So that one might expect the prepostion 'with' to be the one most frequently used?

In a book on linguistics published in 1971 it was contended that it is no longer necessary for people to speak (or write?) in accordance with the rules of traditional grammar books, the rules of which were 'fossilised'. One would like to know whether modern grammar books have superseded the traditional ones and how much licence with the English language is now acceptable. The youth of today may be called upon to be the diplomats of tomorrow, both nationally and internationally. A carefree attitude to grammar in language, whether spoken or written, may have disastrous results.

Apart from problems connected with grammar, the English language has been made more difficult for the average reader by the introduction during the last few decades of new words from the fields of science, medicine, philosophy, etc., not to mention the field of linguistics itself! Has anyone calculated the total of such words invented since the beginning of this century? There are, of course, also, the words borrowed from other languages. The complexities now faced by lexicographers must be immense, but I understand they have the help of computers.

A completely different aspect of language, whether spoken or written, concerns the *quality of thought* it has power to convey. Here is what C. S. Lewis wrote in a letter to Dom. Bede Griffiths:

> 'What an admirable thing it is in the divine economy that the sacred literature of the world' – he had been referring to the Psalms – 'should have been entrusted to a people whose poetry, depending largely on parallelism, should remain poetry in any language you translate it into.'

I was deeply moved on discovering, after my husband's death, a small notebook in which he had jotted down comments after listening to radio and television programmes. On 7th October 1972, he wrote:

> 'In the *Any Questions* programme the view was put forward that Charles Dickens should have used foul language in his novels in order to make them reflect more truly the life of the people of his day.
>
> 'Dickens's aim in writing a book like *A Christmas Carol* was to make people kinder, to make the rich help the poor. He would not have succeeded if he had antagonized his readers by introducing foul language. What is the aim of modern writers? If they have no other aim than to present an authentic picture of sordidness and squalor and perversion, what are they accomplishing? Is it better to have on your table a vase of flowers or a bucket of manure?'[1]

and the same point of view was differently expressed in a letter to *The Listener* of 3rd February 1977, in which it was contended that the degradation of language is the degradation of life.

This train of thought recalls a 'coincidence' which occurred on 7th February 1975. My note reads as follows:

> 'Opened at random Mary Whitehouse's book, which I had brought home from the Library, and read a passage describing her battle with the B.B.C. over *Till Death Us do Part*.

---

[1] In 1989, I am pleased to find the following in Leo McKern's autobiography, *Just Resting*: 'I recently read, and discarded quickly, a projected film script for a Dickens's novel; when I came to the point where one character exclaimed, "You bastard!" I put it down and walked away.'

Night-Scented Stock in Bloom?

'Only an hour later, on the TV *Nationwide* programme, saw people being interviewed about Littlewood's and Vernon's Football Pools, and, suddenly, a fleeting glimpse of "Alf Garnet" was flashed across the screen. He was in Australia! – advertising a football pool, with a few of his usual adjectives thrown in! (My television set had just come back after repair, and I had switched on merely to test it!)'

It seems that people follow trends and fashions in language as they so often do in clothes. I have never understood why capitals are no longer found necessary in the writing of proper names. A coincidence which I noted on 19.10.76 might suggest that the practice involves a kind of 'inverted snobbery'?

'In the country today I watched a little girl writing her name. She wrote her surname beginning with a small letter. I said: "Surely your surname should begin with a capital – the small letter is an Americanism."

'A few hours later when reading, for the first time, *Cranford* by Mrs. Gaskell, I find one of the characters describing her cousin "who spelt his name with two little 'ff's' – ffoulkes – and he always looked down on capital letters (in names)..."!'

Voyagers I and II now travelling in outer space are said to be carrying messages which may not be received there for 1,000 million years. In this case one gathers that 'language' is conveyed by means of objects, illustrations, symbols, etc., it being unlikely that languages used worldwide on our planet have permeated the universe! This demonstrates the idea of the universality of *thought* always taking precedence over language as expressed by the written or spoken word.

We all know that thought is often difficult to put into words. It seems to me that thoughts are presented to us to make of them what we will, using intellectual gifts to the best of our ability. If, as I believe, thought comes from Mind in the universe – the tree of the knowledge of good and evil – which has always been available to man as he emerges gradually into more and more advanced states of consciousness, it is clear that the putting of such thought into words is a process which can never be defined. 'The operations which generate language include processes which cannot be expressed by language' is a quotation from *The Ghost in the Machine*, by Arthur Koestler – which might be reworded to read: 'The operations which generate thought include processes which cannot be *conceived* by thought.'

Speculation about the mysterious world of thought is pursued in further chapters.

Chapter 6

Visions

They're maybe there – who knows how near? –
The visions that we cannot see, the voices that we cannot hear.[1]

The above is an English version of the concluding lines of Vagaland's dialect poem 'Da Sneug Wal'. The poem tells the story of a child – a young boy – who was shown in his dreams where to find healing water which would cure a man who lay helplessly ill with skin sores. It was the dead mother of the sick man who appeared in the boy's dream.

The story is well known in the island of Foula and was related to my husband by friends who lived there. The boy's dream occurred on three consecutive nights. He told a little neighbour girl about it, they followed the directions he had been given, climbed the high hill (Da Sneug) and found the spring exactly as had been described. Is it not possible that the water contained peculiar chemical properties which healed the sick man?

The significance of dreams is something I have never pursued, but I do remember in my young life hearing it said that it was lucky to have one's dreams 'crossed', and I am sure most of us have had some experience of this. One does not always remember a dream on waking, but something may happen during the day to make one recall it. It is a long time since I have had such an experience, and the reason may be that I sleep too soundly! One remarkable experience, however, I do remember, concerning a dream when I was about twenty – more than sixty years ago. The

---

[1] Dey're maybe dere – wha kyins foo near? –
Da veesions at we canna see –
Da voices at we canna hear.
(Vagaland, 'Da Sneug Wal')

dream should have been nightmarish, but I do not recall that it was. In those days, what we called 'the West side steamer' regularly called at Waas, my native village. In my dream I watched it enter our 'voe' or small harbour, and slowly roll over so that I had a full view of the deck, and passengers sliding off it into the sea! When walking up Broughton Street next morning (we were living in Edinburgh at the time) I happened to glance across the way and saw a newspaper placard with the words 'Steamer turns turtle in the Isle of Man'. I hastened to buy a paper, and was relieved to find no lives had been lost. So that was why my dream had not been a nightmare?

Vagaland provided an English rendering of Virgil's poem *'Sunt Geminae Somni Portae'* (There Are Two Gates of Sleep). The middle verse reads:

> Suns that we do not know illuminate
>> The dream-world round us. By their light we see
>> The creatures, bright and dark, of fantasy
> That in the night invade our sleeping state:
> The elfin-folk, the timid unicorn,
>> The nightmare with her goblin train, as she
>> Comes snorting through the gate of ivory.
> – True dreams come quietly through the gate of horn.

I suspect that dreams had particular significance for him. They find their way into other poems, and daydreams, or waking dreams, sometimes gave him a special insight into the past, as in the poem 'Beach of Bright Pebbles', written for our fifth wedding anniversary:

> From earth and air and fire and water made
> The beach lies flooded in soft Summer light;
> The stones forged, shaped, and polished glassy-smooth,
> Milk-white, or topaz-yellow, shining bright
> Among the wash of the receding waves.
> Banded with green, or tinged with red, some lie
> Scattered about upon the pale-gold sand
> Below the misty azure of the sky.
>
> A place to spend a golden afternoon,
> To search, like children, for a pretty stone,
> An ornament, an aid to memory;

44   *Night-Scented Stock in Bloom?*

    And then to feel that we are not alone,
    That there are others with us on this beach
    Not seen, sensed rather in the misty haze,
    Bare-footed, strangely-clad, and searching too
    For hard quartz-pebbles with a gem-bright glaze.

    In days now hidden in the misty past,
    Stones that might make an axe-blade or a knife
    They sought, these others, on the sea-washed shore,
    This beach a bastion in their fight for life.
    Yet sure the beach gave more than toil to them,
    For here they, too, could have a holiday,
    Lie in the sun, their dog forget his flock
    And run along the sand, like ours, at play.

    And doubtless, too, these bare-limbed Stone-age folk,
    Walking like us upon the sun-warmed sand,
    Bathed in the rainbow light of happiness,
    Saw beauty in this summer-scented land;
    Forgot the times of hunger and of cold,
    As we forget the threats of death and wars;
    Felt themselves part of all the pulse of life –
    Night, day, Earth's seasons, and Time's circling stars.

    For me, this is one of his best English poems.[2]
    Mentioned at intervals throughout this work is my neglect of reading. Had I read more, my life might have taken a different course, but this is questionable, given my nature and temperament. At all events, I am able to detect a thread or pattern leading up to the present day, and surely there is now a bonus in the fact that in my declining years there is such a wealth of good literature still to be explored.
    At school, in my day, prizes were still being awarded for attainment or ability. A few years ago I chanced to find on our shelves a book by Kenneth Grahame – *The Golden Age*. It was inscribed with my name and had been awarded for having achieved a mere fifth place in class! The prize was surely undeserved, witness the fact that I had neither then nor

---

[2] 'Beach of Bright Pebbles' was included some years ago in the radio programme *Poetry Please*.

later read the book.[3] There and then I commenced to make good the deficiency.

The reading was briefly interrupted while I prepared lunch. While washing up afterwards, the last verse of one of my husband's poems ran through my mind, for no apparent reason:

> Whin we wir young we dremt aboot a princess
> Sleepin below enchantit waas and tooers;
> An Norwick ida simmer dim is lyin
> Asleep below a twilt at's med o flooers.

Half an hour or so later, reading further through *The Golden Age*, I came to a chapter headed 'The Finding of the Princess'! The narrative included a description of water lilies floating in pools on garden terraces. Water lilies feature in many of my husband's poems.

My practice of writing down such coincidences began in the year in which my husband died. Although more than usually concerned about his health, I must have felt that it would improve as it had so often done before, and, besides, it was a feature of his nature to protect me from concern on his behalf. Looking back it is evident that we were each undergoing deep stress and emotion; it was during this period that we remarked to each other on the strange sequences of events and I decided to write some of them down as they happened.

On one of the last occasions when my husband was able to be out of doors, we visited a shop to buy a newspaper, and, while waiting our turn to be served, he indicated a man a few places in front and said, 'There's Mr. —.' I recognized the man as someone else (in no way resembling Mr. —) but had great difficulty in shaking my husband's conviction that it was indeed his friend. Ten minutes later, after visiting another shop, we returned along the street and whom should we meet but the friend whom my husband had just 'seen', who told us he had newly returned home after some months at sea!

I suggest that in the incident described my husband was undergoing deep emotional stress – he by this time knew there was no cure for his

---

[3] I read somewhere recently that although *The Golden Age* is about children it is hardly a children's book.

---

twilt – quilt; Norwick – the name of a village in Unst where we spent many holidays – is the title of the poem.

illness but kept this knowledge to himself, his stress doubtless being deepened by an awareness that we must soon be parted. I make that statement in all humility for I have never ceased to marvel at his capacity for love. Some time ago I read in a book review that 'we look in poetry for love' and that 'all great poets are more profoundly capable of love than common men'. (These words, of George Sutherland Fraser, were quoted by Cuthbert Graham in the *Aberdeen Press and Journal* of 1st October 1977.) Vagaland was a true poet, and I think this will some day be more widely recognized. This view was in some way strengthened by an experience on 29th October 1976. While busy at the kitchen sink (many of my 'thoughts' came to me there!) I recalled that, when I decided to publish the collected poems, I had said that if not fully appreciated now they would come into their own in the next century. In our lending library, an hour later, I glanced through the pages of a book called *English Poetry – a Short History* by Kenneth Hopkins and found myself reading the following:

> 'but Byron himself, commenting on the fact that he wrote "The Corsair" in ten days and "The Bride of Abydos" in only four (this last sold six thousand copies in the first month following publication) added that "such things . . . cannot have stamina for permanent attention". This is the proper verdict on almost all poetry popular in its day, for the very qualities that make for wide immediate popularity are those least likely to carry a work over into another generation, and another century.'

I borrowed Kenneth Hopkins's book from the Library and found in it other interesting observations which are quoted elsewhere to support a viewpoint or opinion.

Chapter 7

Vagaland and Housman

When reading the biography of A. E. Housman, by Richard Perceval Graves, I encountered a quotation from Housman's *'Diffugere Nives'*, which reminded me that Vagaland wrote a dialect translation of the same Horace Ode (Book IV, Ode 7):

    Noo at da Winter snaa is geen fae da hill an vailley
        Da green paeck comes agyin;
    Every burn an stripe is brokken his frosty tedder
        An doon ta da ebb dey rin.

    Glansin wings ida lift – da speerit o Spring, da Tirrik!
        An sweet da laverik's sang.
    Less, foo da shangin year is a warnin ta everybody
        At naethin lests fir lang.

    Mairch caald shön gies wye ta da sun an da rain in April;
        Da Dim owercomes da Voar.
    Hairst comes gallopin on, an, afore du kyins, da Winter
        Is back afore dy door.

    Mön aye follows mön, dey're wanin an dan dey're growin,
        Bit folk, O less-a-less,
    Kings an möld-rich men, an aa at's apo da Fit-stöl,
        Dir end is dust an ess.

Wha can ever tell, whin he lays him doon at nicht-faa
If he'll braethe da moarnin air.
Mak da best o dis wirld: du taks no a thing ta da next een
Da naked sowl gengs dere.

Eftir du's geen awa, ta da place at aa-man gengs til,
Dan nedder freend or kin,
Or onything at du's döne in aa da years o dy lifetime,
Can bring dee back agyin.

Nedder da love at da laad can lay afore his sweethert,
Or a man gie til his wife,
Or da haand o da truest freend, can draa fae da idder wirld
A boddie back ta life.

The above is a somewhat freer translation than that of Housman, whose poetry Vagaland so much admired, but to anyone familiar with the dialect (and perhaps even to those coming to it for the first time) it is clear that the spirit of the original has been preserved and interpreted with fluency and rhythm. It was Edward Marsh who said that it was 'obvious that the only way to translate' (poetry) 'is to get a good grasp of the author's thought and feeling and then recast it according to the genius of one's own language.' (See *Ambrosia and Small Beer* by Christopher Hassall.)

The term 'scholar-poet' which Graves has applied to Housman could with justice be applied to Vagaland. Despite the most severe financial restrictions in childhood and adulthood, and deprivations which at times reduced standards of living to mere subsistence, if not near starvation, levels, he acquired an education which would stand comparison with any provided by our present-day welfare state, with its educational opportunities for all. At University in Edinburgh he specialised in English and History (subjects which he later taught), but he had a natural 'flair' for languages, and in the last two years of his life he began a study of Greek (self-taught) which had not been part of his school curriculum.

In his fourth year at Lerwick Secondary School, which is now known as the Anderson High School, Vagaland had the distinction of securing a prize for being 'the best scholar-athlete'. He excelled in the high jump,

---

green paeck – first green of Spring; stripe – small stream; tirrik – tern; laverik – skylark; Da (simmer) Dim – symbol of summer; Voar – spring; less-a-less – alas! alas!; möld-rich – very wealthy; Fit-stöl – the earth; ess – ashes; aa-man – everybody; nedder – neither.

according to his school friends, one of whom presented me with a small snapshot, taken by herself, which captured evidence of one of his mighty leaps, well clear of the cross-bar! Alas, his athletic activities were curtailed in the following years because of a bout of glandular fever which, in my opinion, may have caused a deficiency in health from which he never fully recovered.

The series *Poems of Today* introduced us to contemporary poetry in those far-off schooldays, and it may have been then that my husband's love of Housman's poetry was born. Some thirty years later, when staying with friends in Bromsgrove,[1] he found himself in the heart of the countryside which had given birth to one of his favourite poets. This was before our marriage, but a year or so later we visited Bromsgrove together and I sensed how much Housman's poetry meant to him at that time. His mother's long illness, her suffering and death only a year or two previously, may, I now believe, have caused him to have a strong 'rapport' with much that was written in 'A Shropshire Lad', and subsequently in *The Collected Poems of A. E. Housman*, of which I see his copy is the Tenth Impression published in 1949.

At that time my own interest in the poems of Housman was confined chiefly to those included in the song cycles composed by George Butterworth, and we never missed an opportunity of listening to any which were included in radio broadcasts.

My husband was a teacher by profession – an exacting one for him. There is little doubt that his abilities and qualifications could have been used to much greater advantage in other fields, such as literary research and the development of his poetic gifts for which his teaching duties left so little time. Over a long period of years classes were abnormally large, often over forty in number, and, with homework as the rule, there was always a mass of correcting work to be done. At examination time, and, indeed, frequently throughout the school term, our sitting-room floor would of an evening be strewn with papers! There was thus less time than one could have wished for him to pursue private interests and develop his undoubted gifts. A true assessment of his qualities is contained in the tribute paid by a former headmaster in an address to the Zetland Education Committee:

---

[1] Vagaland actually wrote a poem about Housman which he sent to R. K. Morcom, The Clock House, Bromsgrove, after his visit to Housman country in 1951. No copy exists here.

'I had the privilege during most of his teaching career of being able to assess and appreciate the many qualities that Mr. Robertson had, both as a teacher and as a person. I think I am safe in saying that it would be very hard to find anywhere a person or a teacher who came to his work in such a conscientious spirit, who gave sympathetic consideration to the children under his charge, and who gave such a loyalty both to this authority, to the school and to his colleagues. His overriding concern was always the welfare and progress of his pupils. This community will remember Mr. Robertson as one of Shetland's most outstanding poets. His love of Shetland, his profound knowledge of the Shetland dialect, his awareness of the beauties of nature, and of nature in all its moods, is very ably expressed and vividly illustrated in all his poems.'

However, in spite of the demands which teaching made, Vagaland read as widely as possible, obtaining books on request from the local library, and reading newspapers, with special interest in book reviews. (Incidentally, over a long period of years until he retired, he provided the series *Pictorial Education* for the schoolchildren.) It may safely be said that, after giving whatever help he could in house or garden, he was seldom to be seen seated without a book in his hand. But his reading to the best of my knowledge did not often include biographies and one feels he would have considered it an intrusion to delve too deeply into the private lives of other people. As an indication of this, the letters we exchanged during my breakdown were destroyed by mutual consent. We destroyed mine many years ago, preserving his until, on our removal to this house in 1970, he suggested they should also be destroyed. In many ways I am sorry I agreed, for they could only have served as an additional record of the beauty and constancy of his nature.

I have not read the previous biographies of Alfred Housman, nor do I know whether my husband read any of them. I do not think his visits to Bromsgrove forty years ago were concerned with interests other than the poet's environment, and, indeed, judging from the book *Bromsgrove and the Housmans* by John Pugh, published in 1974, the interest still centres on the poetry so far as the people of Bromsgrove are concerned.

I write with some confidence here, for it was as a result of reading a review of a biography of J. M. Barrie that my husband was constrained to write his poem 'J. M. B.'. The review had apparently indicated the biographer's conclusion that Barrie 'was not the same as other men'. Here are the last two verses of Vagaland's poem:

> Barrie for half a century and more
> Has yearly opened an enchanted door
> To Fairyland for many a girl and boy,
> A door that led to pleasure and to joy.
> I like to think that some of those, who died,
> Were waiting for him on the other side,
> For he was not the same as other men;
>
> And that this man, at times both sad and lone,
> With all the children who have never known
> The agony, the pain and bitter strife,
> Nor yet the ecstasy of adult life,
> With those untimely laid beneath the sod,
> Has grown and flowered in the green fields of God
> In every way the same as other men.

In his biography of Rupert Brooke, Christopher Hassall quoted from a letter by Rupert Brooke to Geoffrey Keynes: 'Yesternight I was vastly happy. I saw Peter Pan. It was perfect. It is merely and completely the incarnation of all one's childish dreams – the best dreams, almost, that one has. . . .'

'*Diffugere Nives*' was not the only Horace Ode translated by Vagaland into the Shetland dialect. In 1959, Ronald Storrs produced his book *Ad Pyrrham* – A Polyglot Collection of Translations of Horace's Ode to Pyrrha (Book 1, Ode V). In *The New Shetlander* No. 50 Vagaland's version was introduced in these words;

> "'Possibly the first 'dumb blonde' mentioned in literature was a yellow-haired young woman who lived about two thousand years ago. A poet addressed her in an immortal ode." Thus Moray McLaren introduced a recent article on Horace's famous ode *Ad Pyrrham* which has the amazing distinction of existing in over 450 translations, in at least 26 languages . . . McLaren . . . notes with regret that there is none in any dialect of Scots. Vagaland has decided to remedy this defect at once, and now adds a very Shetland Kirstie to "the monstrous regiment" of Pyrrhas who

have wantoned their way down the centuries, from Horace's day to ours. . . .'

Ad Pyrrham

(From Horace, Book 1, Ode V)

What boannie laad, his broo-hair sleekit back,
Coorts wi dee noo ita da restin-shair,
Kirstie, my lass? Fir what een o da baand
Sits du sae lang ta redd dy golden hair?

Less, less, I doot he'll fin at du can shange
As da sea shanges ida Simmer Dim.
Pör sowl, he tinks du haes a hert o gold
An trusts, göd feth, du'll aye be true ta him;

Sae he sails on, firyattin foo a gael
Fae a black calm can spring apo da sea.
Nae man sood ever trust a Joolie sky
An, less, he'll fin at hit's da sam wi dee!

A'm faced da sea ita my time, hit's true;
Bit whin da wadder gets ower coorse, I wat,
A man jöst haes ta hing his oilskin up,
Geng inbee ta da fire, an set him at!

It was a surprise to read in the biography by Graves that Housman had visited Scotland, staying in a country house in Ardtornish which overlooks the Sound of Mull, and it was a delight to discover that he had seen there for the first time the Grass of Parnassus. This dainty little flower grows also in isolated spots in Shetland and is known by the name 'White Kaitrin'. A line from another Horace Ode introduces the Vagaland poem 'Da Wal Gaet', with its nostalgic memories of these 'White Kaitrins':

---

redd – comb; less, less – alas, alas; firyattin – forgetting; set (him) at – settle comfortably (and, here, resignedly as well!), cf. Nor. 'baere seg at'.

Vagaland and Housman

'*O fons Bandusiae, splendidior vitro.*'

(From Horace, Ode XIII)

Aald Roman poet, A'm blyde ta read dy verses
   An best o aa, I laek ta hear dee sing
Aboot da aik tree growin aside da water
   At bubbled clear fae dy Bandusian spring.

I come in mind o a wal at da daeks o Gröntoo
   Whaar I wid geng fir water years ago,
Alang da burra rodd ida Simmer hömin,
   Whin stillness lay ower hill an loch an voe.

Whin aa wis dry wi lang, haet days in Joolie,
   Da Gröntoo wal wis aalwis lipperin foo,
An whaar da water wimpled ower da mödow,
   Here an dere da peerie White Kaitrins grew.

An folk wis wint ta geng wi widden daffiks
   Fir mony a fraacht, whin da Simmer nicht wid faa,
Or geng, tired oot wi da dadderie o Voar time,
   Or brak a brod ta da wal trowe fanns o snaa.

Der little need nooadays fir pails or daffiks.
   You turn a tap, an da water comes itsell;
Bit, lass, der somethin geen at we ill can pairt wi,
   An what dat is we canna richtly tell.

Bit da wal still rins, as bricht an clear as ever,
   Though Time, Göd kyins, is altered mony a thing.
An I tink we'll geng – we're bön ower lang awa, lass–
   An see da White Kaitrins growin aside da spring.

---

blyde – glad; aik – oak; wal – well; daeks – dykes; burra rodd – heath road; hömin – twilight; haet – hot; Joolie – July; aalwis – always; lipperin foo – brimming over; wimpled – rippled; mödow – meadow; peerie – small; wint – wont; widden – wooden; daffik – wooden water pail; fraacht – burden; dadderie – drudgery; brak a brod – make a path; fann – snowdrift; we're bön – we have been.

Chapter 8

The Catalyst

'Speaking not figuratively but literally, it may be said that love, being the most powerful of all emotions, unveils in the soul of man all its qualities patent and latent; and it may also unfold those new potencies which even now constitute the object of occultism and mysticism – the development of powers in the human soul so deeply hidden that by the majority of men their very existence is denied.'
(Ouspensky, quoted by Fritz Peters in his book on Gurdjieff)

The older and biblical word for love is, of course, 'charity', comparative definitions of which are:

Love of fellow men; kindness, affection; leniency in judging others (*Concise Oxford Dictionary*, 1976)
Love of God and of one's neighbour (*Nouveau Petit Larousse*, 1924)

For the purpose of my theme, which is that man's first allegience is to God, who is Love – as recognised and expressed 3,000 years ago in the First Commandment – it would be reassuring to find that the modern Larousse still gives the above definition of '*charité*'.

It is my belief that love is the catalyst which produces the mysterious occurrence of visions. A few days after my husband's death, while sitting by the fireside I dozed briefly and, on awakening, had the amazing experience of seeing him seated opposite me, re-united with our little dog, the two greeting each other with the utmost affection. Our dog, Susie, had died some years before and had never lived in our new house, to which we moved in 1970.

Susie features in an anniversary poem written by Vagaland in 1956:

Widwick[1]

The wind-blown mist drove in o'er Widwick,
   Over the strand where wreckage lay –
Planks and logs and spars and battens,
   Storm-spoil gathered many a day.

Nothing stirred in the lonely hollow,
   But a heron startled into flight;
The great grey crag rose high above us,
   Looming up in the misty light.

We lay on the green turf there and rested,
   Watching the fitful sunlight shine,
And climbed to look for garnets, sprinkled
   Over the rock like drops of wine.

And Summer winds that blow o'er Houlland,
   Will see us come again, us three,
Down the sheep-track into Widwick,
   You and the Susie dog and me.

For years I have pondered over the miracle of my 'vision', and always I conclude that it occurred as a result of my having so often seen my husband seated opposite me by the fireside, after lunch, in our previous home, snatching a few minutes respite before returning to afternoon duty. But I distinctly remember one particular occasion when, as I watched him thus, with our little dog at his side, my whole being was suffused with love.

Surely it was a bond of mutual love that made it possible for Christ to appear to so many of his followers after his death on the Cross. This could also explain Paul's experience on the road to Damascus, for deep down in his heart he must have been aware of Christ's love – had most likely seen him addressing the crowds and was no doubt haunted by this memory while he persisted in persecuting Christ's followers.

---

[1] Widwick – a secluded cove or inlet in the island of Unst, Shetland.

It could also explain the incidents on the road to Emmaeus. In their emotional state the two disciples could well have been given a vision of Jesus in the breaking of the bread.

Viewed in this way the story of Christ's resurrection presents no difficulty for me. When reading the Gospels one has to take into account that they were written several years after Christ's death on the cross, and written at a time when people clung to many pagan beliefs; and the gospel writers, in recording that Christ had 'appeared' to his many beloved followers, in some cases caused their readers to assume that this was a bodily resurrection. On the other hand there are passages in the narratives which make it clear that the 'appearances' were far from being 'physical', for Christ 'appeared through closed doors', or 'vanished from their sight'.

I felt one day in 1976 that my interpretation of these New Testament accounts was being miraculously supported by another strange 'coincidence'. The 'coincidences' – for want of a better name – happening regularly after my husband's death, were so extraordinary that I recorded them as they occurred. My notebook entry on 7th October 1976, reads:

> 'In double-glazed windows strange reflections can occur. While working at the kitchen sink this morning, I observed, reflected in the window, the kitchen door swinging open behind me (it does this often, because the floor level is not true!). The reflection showed the door *swinging through* another (cupboard) door which was standing open. I thought of the Gospel passage which told of Christ appearing through a closed door.
>
> 'An hour or so later when reading *The Crystal Cave* (by Mary Stewart), a book recently recommended to me by a friend in Wales, I was astonished to find Merlin saying: "I am not the kind that can walk through walls, and bring bodies through locked doors."'

It is now recognized by many that experiences such as these are the lot of people undergoing emotional stress, or who are emotionally disturbed. In this connection, I refuse to accept, except in a limited sense, the term 'mentally disturbed'. There is a subtle difference. Admittedly, we have, during the last half century at least, been living in an age which has tended to despise any expression of emotion, and the mind has been regarded as a machine – an outcome of the age of mechanism – a machine whose 'software' fed into computers will one day produce 'Super Intelligence'! But can there be Intelligence devoid of feeling, compassion and emotion?

The 'software' fed into computers may in some way have been influenced by the feelings, etc., of individuals, but the computer, being a machine, cannot itself be similarly influenced.

To define 'emotion' as 'moving of the feelings' (Chambers' *Twentieth Century Dictionary*, 1937) is, in my opinion, preferable to the definition 'disturbance of the mind' (*Concise Oxford Dictionary*) although, in a limited sense only, deep emotion – caused by the death of a loved one, for example – may cause the mind to be 'disturbed' to the extent that completely new *insights* into the meaning of life, and death, can present themselves and be accepted. In this situation new wavelengths seem to be available for the entry of thoughts. But where do these thoughts come from? My conclusion is that those who have gone before are permitted to communicate with us – a belief surely held by the church down the ages when referring to the 'communion of saints'. Two verses from a hymn, 'For those we love within the veil', by William Charter Piggott (1872–1943), occur to me:

> O, fuller, sweeter is that life
> And larger, ampler is the air;
> Eye cannot see nor heart conceive
> The glory there;
>
> Nor know to what high purpose Thou
> Dost yet employ their ripened powers
> Nor how at Thy behest they touch
> This life of ours.

Only recently did I discover that the writer of these words was one and the same person as the minister whose church I attended some sixty years ago in London!

The subject of spiritualism has never attracted me. This may be due in some part to my upbringing, but it would never occur to me to try to make contact with those from whom death has parted us. My faith urges me to make all prayers direct to the God of Love, whose power, I believe, will support us in whatever situation we find ourselves. I think my husband's life on earth would have been conducted on the same basis of faith, though it may surprise some readers to know this was a topic on which we rarely conversed. On the other hand, the strength of his faith was adequately revealed in his poetry and by the way he lived. Undoubtedly he lived by a code of Christian ethics, applied strictly to himself in his dealings with others. And he had the poet's mysticism which gave him a special awareness of a hidden world which confronts us every now and then with the inexplicable. Speculation about the mysterious world of thought must have led him to write the following poem during his last illness:

Night-scented Stock[2]

On soundless wings the voyagers of night-time
    Who need no guiding light upon their way
Steer through uncharted air to find a haven
    Of rest at dusk of day.

The scent of flowers, by unseen pathways carried,
    Has brought them safely through a deep of gloom,
To find, within the quiet of the garden,
    Night-scented stock in bloom.

When we are growing old, and deepening shadows
    Blot out the path where we have wandered far,
When we know not the place to which we journey,
    Unlit by moon or star;

The thoughts of others who have truly loved us
    May flow towards us on the channelled air,
Guiding us to a place beyond the darkness,
    To find a garden there.

I have indicated my own attitude to spiritualism. Conclusions reached by W. R. Matthews, a former Dean of St. Paul's, in his autobiographical *Memories and Meanings*, are contained in the words: '. . . it is entirely rational and necessary to study psychical phenomena in the context of religion and to consider whether the needs which are met by spiritualism cannot be met by a deeper understanding of the communion of the saints.'

    Not long ago, in a radio 'phone-in' programme, one speaker was derided because he put forward as an obvious solution to the troubles in Northern Ireland that a 'change of heart' was required. He was right, of

---

[2] These flowers were among those he raised from seed in the garden of our new home in 1973. The voyagers of night-time are, of course, the nocturnal insects.

The Catalyst

course, for the 'change of heart' involves recognition of the transforming power of love – first and foremost a genuine love of God, which should mean 'loving Him with all one's heart, soul, strength and mind'. Without God, man is powerless to solve the world's problems. When man's solutions fail, having relied on schemes independently devised (that is, devised without love), he turns to violence with its inevitably disastrous results for guilty and innocent alike. The plight of refugees, shown on TV during the war in Nigeria some years ago, evoked this compassionate protest from the pen of Vagaland:

> Laek fleein swaabies, seekin
> fir maet oot ower da klak,
> Sae seeks, firever restless,
> da herts at's laek ta brak.
> Laek fleein spöndrift, scattered
> in froad apo da taing
> Da sowls o folk at's hattered
> in end fae life sall geng.
>
> Bit laek da weary haaf-man,
> oot-woarn, an seekin haem,
> Dey'll get da Eart, dir midder
> ta mak a place fir dem.
> Whin Death dir lot sall alter,
> ta rest at last dey'll win;
> Da sea-fool he finns shalter –
> da sea in end sall linn.

---

swaabie – great black-backed gull; klak – a great stone or rock; spöndrift – spindrift; froad – foam; taing – flat land projecting into the sea; hattered – oppressed; haaf-man – deep sea fisherman; midder – mother; win ta – reach; sea-fool – sea-bird; linn – rest, abate.

Chapter 9

'Gleanings from a Navvy's Scrapbook'

Love will live while the pale stars glow, while the world shall last,
On the present hopes, and in hours of woe, on a dreamy past,
Love will live, while the flowers bloom and the meadows wave,
Nor yet be quenched by the charnel tomb or the ghastly grave.
For o'er the tomb and the silver stars, to the gates above
The soul will seek in the great afar the endless Love.

The words are by the Irish poet, Patrick MacGill (1891–1963), and I met them by chance when cataloguing my husband's books a year or two after his death. A line by Southey appears above the poem – 'They sin who tell us love can die'.

Songs of the Dead End, a collection of poems by Patrick MacGill, was first published in 1913, and has a foreword by Canon Dalton, the then archivist of Windsor Castle, who tells us that 'MacGill, when twelve years old, was engaged as a farm hand in the Irish Midlands, where his work began at five o'clock in the morning and went on till eleven at night through summer and winter. It was a man's work with a boy's pay. At fourteen, seeking newer fields, he crossed from 'Derry to Scotland and there, for seven years, was either a farm hand, drainer, tramp, hammerman, navvy, platelayer or wrestler.'

According to information given in *A Dictionary of Irish Biography*, which I consulted in our local library, MacGill's first publication was *Gleanings from a Navvy's Scrapbook* (c.1911) and included translations of La Fontaine's Fables and Goethe's poems.

Having spent his young life as a casual labourer, MacGill dedicated his *Songs of the Dead End* to his 'pick and shovel'. With the poetic gift he undoubtedly had, what might he not have achieved from further education at college or university? Indeed, even his elementary school education must have been limited, as he was the eldest of a family of eleven for whom he was expected to help to provide.

The impact of his poetry on the contemporary literary scene was quite startling, to judge from quotations from press reviews of *Songs of the Dead End*. For example, *The Pall Mall Gazette*, *The Bookman*, *The Clarion*, *The Cambridge Review*, *The Poetry Review* and *The Star* commented respectively, in these words: 'verses of remarkable vigour'; 'work of real genius'; 'he can do things, can our navvy poet'; 'thrice over has he earned his right to a goodly heritage'; 'work of human interest'; 'the greatest poet since Kipling'.

However, *The Church Times* withheld praise in the words, 'Has not English poetry, with all its splendid traditions, a higher message for the time than this?' and *The Manchester Guardian* was 'at a loss to understand what manner of youth he is'.

On reading *Children of the Dead End*, an autobiographical novel by MacGill, there comes a full understanding of the conditions which led him to write as he did about the casual labourer's life at the beginning of this century. I have not read any more of his work, which included plays as well as verse. The style of the latter is indeed reminiscent of Kipling, and possibly also of Robert Service. It appears he wrote no more after 1930 and spent the latter part of his life in America.

The television series *Life on Earth* would have fascinated MacGill, whose interest was expressed in 'A Geological Nightmare':

> But where are they gone to, the mammoth and auk?
>   The dodo and dragon, say, where are they gone?
> In the Triassic beds and the Eocene chalk
>   They have fallen asleep and are slumbering on.
> The knight of the sickle has numbered their days,
>   And nature embalmed them in shells and in stones,
> And we, their descendants, in boundless amaze,
>   Discuss them or pore o'er their fossilized bones.

His resistance to suppression of his literary gifts is apparent in these lines:

> There are lots of folks who clamour that the man who
>   strikes the hammer cannot, though he'd like to, rise
> From the squalor of the masses to the glory of Parnassus
>   (which, I might remark, is lies).

His humour can be found in:

> I am one of those who know it, it takes more to make a poet
> Than a mass of flowing hair.

His philosophy or faith in such lines as:

> My floor the earth, my roof the sky,
> And God Himself the Architect.

and

> For we are brothers one and all,
>   Some day we'll know through Heaven's grace,
> And then the drudge will find a place
>   Beside the master of the hall.

Whatever his merits as a poet, the verse quoted at the beginning of this chapter emphasises the theme which I try to develop throughout these pages.

Chapter 10

The Welfare State

Nowadays, in this country, responsibility for care of the elderly has largely been transferred from the individual to the state. Has this been an unmixed blessing? The need to make provision for a 'rainy day' is not so pressing as it was for our parents and grandparents. In my childhood days, the Old Age pension was seven shillings and sixpence per week! In Shetland, in those days, elderly parents, no longer able to take an active part in the work of the home, or on the land, lived out their days in their own homes, cared for by their families. In turn, grandchildren had their love and care, and for the most part reciprocated with love and respect. Could it not be that the present trends of the welfare state to separate the generations – grandparents, parents, and sometimes children, will lead to even more pronounced 'generation gaps' than can already frequently be seen to exist?

Immediately after writing the foregoing, I watched the film star, Sophia Loren, being interviewed on television by Donny MacLeod, and learned that in her autobiography she had emphasised how important family ties were to her, especially in conditions of extreme poverty. She described her devotion to her grandmother, whom she still thought of as her 'guardian angel'.

Of course, there are many cases of elderly people living alone, who prefer to maintain their independence – my own case is an example. One would hope that so long as we do not prove to be a burden on our neighbours (and here again mutual love and respect will decide) we may be allowed to live out our lives in dignity and a degree of independence.

Love and caring in the sphere of nursing was a theme touched upon a few years ago in a radio programme which asked why it was that in so many hospitals there was at that time a shortage of nurses. One view was that the nursing services were underpaid, but that did not seem to be the full explanation. We were told by one of the speakers that almost any small girl, when asked what she would like to be when she grows up, will reply unhesitatingly 'a Nurse'. No doubt the attractive dress usually worn by nurses explains part of the appeal to the child, but I think it may go deeper than this. The natural instinct to love and care, and, sometimes, even a willingness to make sacrifices, is often there in the child, demanding to be satisfied.

The love and caring instinct in the animal world should give us cause to reflect. I recently rediscovered the following 'haiku' written by my husband:

Love

A bird trails her wing
In the path of the weasel
that fledglings may sing.

Another opinion expressed in the radio discussion was that in hospital nursing as it used to be there was more opportunity (and time?) to express love and compassion. Modern medical treatment seems to be introducing more and more 'mechanised' nursing (the adjective is my own) and hospitals have their 'intensive care' units which demand very special types of skill.

Could not also the shortage of nurses in some cases be accounted for by doubts about the ethics of abortions, genetic engineering, organ transplants. etc., etc.?

My husband in his last illness was enough concerned about modern trends in medicine (disclosed by radio and TV programmes) to leave a few comments in a small notebook which he kept by his side. This is what he wrote on 11th August 1973:

'If the various kinds of equipment used to prolong human life multiply much more, and if there are more and more organ transplants, it is not difficult to imagine a world where parts of the population are permanently attached to kidney machines or heart machines, while others are turned into zombies – living dead animated by spare parts taken from corpses.

'No one' (on the radio programme) 'suggested that it would be better to spend money and valuable time in the study of preventive medicine.'

The thought has just occurred to me: 'In the case of heart or other organ transplants, when does the body of a donor become a corpse?'

I would add an additional comment that preventive medicine might first be practised in those areas of the world which are being deprived of the bare necessities of life, and where the main problem is malnutrition. One reads that in the year 1975 there were in Bangladesh 75,000,000 people, 8,000 doctors and less than 1,000 trained nurses.

In the sphere of preventive medicine, also, diligent research might be pursued to discover what may be the long-term effects of the heavy consumption of alcohol in our present age? If alcohol can have such damaging effects on the brain of the one who over-indulges in it, what may not be the effect on his or her descendants? Has this possibility been thoroughly explored and studied? The dangers inherent in excessive wine drinking have been recognized since earliest recorded times, and undoubtedly the introduction of strong spirits in recent centuries has greatly increased the problem. Dr. Erasmus Darwin (grandfather of Charles Darwin) writing in the eighteenth century believed that all the 'drunken diseases' were hereditary in some degree, and that epilepsy and insanity were originally produced by drinking. (See his letter to his son, in *The Autobiography of Charles Darwin*.) Was it simple observation that led writers in biblical times to remark that the sins of the fathers are visited unto the third and fourth generation? If there is any truth in the observation, why has there not been as big a campaign to control drinking habits as has been conducted against cigarette smoking, now believed to be a cause of lung cancer?

Alcoholism is now being described in some quarters as a 'disease'. This is, I think, a dangerous attitude to adopt, implying that it is something that simply happens to people. Is it suggested that human will-power no longer plays a part in human behaviour? On the other hand, the implication may be that alcoholism is one of the 'diseases' which man, by his own actions, inflicts upon himself.

At the time of my writing the above, a doctor stated on radio: 'There are now 100,000 "problem drinkers" in Scotland.'

If the disastrous effects of excessive smoking and drinking are perhaps only fully revealed in succeeding generations, here is a sphere for 'preventive medicine', a sphere in which every individual person can act to protect the health of posterity. Have we not all heard of the calamities which have befallen peoples of the world to whom alcohol has been introduced? For this influence the so-called civilized western world may one day be called to account. This is not a situation in which the individual can claim to be powerless, leaving decision and responsibility to others. Power and responsibility lie with each one of us.

Anything which has the effect of impairing mental powers and judgment, an effect evident in anyone 'under the influence', surely cannot be said to be good for either the individual himself or for humanity in general. On radio and television we are sometimes invited to take comfort from the fact that the 'U.K. is not the "heaviest drinking" country in Europe or the world.' (But what does this prove? Are we trying to get into the Guinness Book of Records?) On other occasions we are told that serious drink problems occur in situations of great affluence as well as of great poverty, so that the solution of the drink problem does not necessarily lie in the improvement of living conditions.

Has a study been made of the incidence of cancer and other diseases in countries whose people are not addicted to alcohol consumption?

Much more could be said, such as that 'alcoholism is the biggest killer on the road' (radio news 14.8.79). Clear thinking can only operate when the intellect is in peak control. When it is known that alcohol and drugs impair this control, leading to an increase in road accidents, violence, sex abuse, and so on, man cannot plead ignorance of his individual responsibility, possibly for the whole future of the human race.

Chapter 11

The Pursuit of Knowledge

'... My mind seems to have become a kind of machine for grinding general laws out of large collections of facts, but why this should have caused the atrophy of that part of the brain alone on which the higher tastes depend I cannot conceive. . . . The loss of these tastes is a loss of happiness, and may possibly be injurious to the intellect, and more probably to the moral character, by enfeebling the emotional part of our nature.'
(The Autobiography of Charles Darwin)

In *The Diary of Beatrice Webb* (edited by Norman and Jeanne Mackenzie) there is a reference to the 'mental deformity which results from the extraordinary development of the intellectual faculties, joined with the very imperfect development of the sympathetic and emotional qualities'. It does seem possible that total devotion to study, research or intellectual activity of any kind, to the exclusion of sympathetic human contacts, may result in a diminution of the emotional capacity for love on which all human happiness finally depends.

In his Reith lectures 1976, published in *The Listener*, 2nd December 1976, Colin Blakemore spoke of the evolution of ideas in human culture which would originally have come about by a gradual process of natural selection: 'In general, useful ideas would survive because they would propagate themselves just as an adaptive genetic mutation flourishes. Ideas which proved worthless would gradually be discarded and forgotten. It seems that all this has been changed by the emergence of a "kind of communal intellect – the collective mind of man", which since the invention of printing, magnetic tape and computer cards, has 'lost the vital ability to forget'. I quote from these Reith Lectures because they seem to emphasise the sense of misgiving expressed by Darwin about a century ago. Colin Blakemore's words concluded with the warning: 'He'. . . (man) . . . 'might simply drown himself in a flood of information; society could collapse because it no longer comprehends its cultural inheritance.

'To know all knowledge leaves the truth unknown', and it may be time for man to pause and take stock of where his 'knowledge' may be leading him.

I find it impossible to accept the suggestion made by Arthur Koestler, in his book *The Ghost in the Machine*, that there is what might be called a flaw in the evolution of man's brain, and that the older and primitive brain – the part now said to be involved with his emotions – is responsible for man's irrational actions. The truth is surely that man's emotions are as essential to his well-being as his intellect, and emotions and intellect must interact as a harmonious whole. Of especial interest are these concluding words of Professor J. Bronowski in his television series *The Ascent of Man*: 'The intellectual equipment and the emotional equipment, working together as one, has made the Ascent of Man.'

However, control of passions such as anger, jealousy, hate, etc., can only be maintained by appealing to all-conquering Love. In a broadcast Quaker service on 27th January 1980, this wise comment was made: 'Anger must be there but it must be controlled by Love that evil cannot stir.'

It seems to me that these lines by Francis Bourdillon (1852–1921) can be applied to the life of the whole of mankind:

> The night has a thousand eyes
>   And the day but one
> Yet the light of the bright world dies
>   With the dying sun.
> The mind has a thousand eyes
>   And the heart but one,
> But the light of the whole life dies
>   When love is done.

Is it not possible that man, now tending to rely on his intellect alone to provide him with all possible knowledge about himself, the world and the universe, is more and more shutting himself off from his only source of happiness, his God of Love – Love the Catalyst on which the very survival of humanity depends.

Chapter 12

Patriotism

In an earlier chapter I quoted lines from Walter de la Mare:

> Look thy last on all things lovely
> ....
> ....
> Since that all things thou would'st praise
> Beauty took from those who loved them
> In other days.

The concluding lines of 'The Great Lover', by Rupert Brooke, might have been quoted in the same context:

> O dear my loves, O faithless, once again
> This one last gift I give: that after men
> Shall know, and later, lovers, far-removed,
> Praise you, 'All these were lovely'; say, 'He loved.'

It is sad that so many of those who achieved success and distinction in their lifetime are now made to emerge as lesser figures at the hands of their biographers. Rupert Brooke is only one among many who have suffered in this way. I have been reading John Lehmann's *Rupert Brooke – his Life and his Legend*, in which I consider an unjust comparison is made between Brooke's essentially pre-war poetry and the war poetry of such poets as Wilfred Owen and Siegfried Sassoon, whose direct experience of the horrors and carnage of trench warfare led them to write so differently.

Rupert Brooke's poetry, where the decried sonnets are concerned, is the poetry of patriotism, but was not this the spirit of his age? On television,

Lord Brockway, at the age of ninety-two, a lifelong socialist, expressed the opinion that the actions of the people of any nation will always in the last resort be governed by patriotism! Although it is increasingly obvious that we peoples of the earth must learn to stop thinking of ourselves in terms of nationhood, it is doubtful whether we have yet taken to heart the observation of Nurse Edith Cavell in the 1914–1918 war that 'patriotism is not enough'.

Brooke is said to have had a 'puritan upbringing', which may or may not be true, because it is difficult to know at what stage standards of any kind must be described as 'puritan'. There is little doubt that he tried to adhere to his own innate moral code, which at times led to much heart-searching, as a number of his letters reveal. As we go through life it is normal for most of us to develop a 'conscience' which derives, I believe, from inner truths which we have grown to recognize and acknowledge.

Much emphasis has been laid on 'his great physical beauty', 'his extraordinary magnetic charm', etc., which John Lehmann thinks may have supported and enhanced the effect of the sonnets, but seventy-odd years ago readers throughout the country could know little of these qualities, and Virginia Woolf, a friend of Rupert Brooke, in a sensitive tribute, did not emphasise his 'personal beauty'. She speaks of him being 'conventionally handsome and English'.

The last long Fragment, quoted by John Lehmann as having been written by Rupert Brooke in the Aegean shortly before he died, makes it clear that he was only too aware of the awful magnitude of the sacrifices about to be made in the First World War. During his illness on board the troopship, one gathers he was able at times to obtain glimpses of his men:

> No one could see me.
> I would have thought of them
> – Heedless, within a week of battle – in pity,
> Pride in their strength and in the weight and firmness
> And link'd beauty of bodies, and pity that
> This gay machine of splendour'ld soon be broken,
> Thought little of, pashed, scattered . . .

We cannot begin to imagine the effects on his writing of possible subsequent war experiences, had he survived.

Before discovering among my husband's books a few years ago a collection of poems entitled *A Letter to Lucian*, I had not read any of the work of Alfred Noyes, but I became interested enough to ask our local library to obtain on loan his autobiography *Two Worlds for Memory*. This came to hand on the very day on which I returned to our library the book written by John Lehmann. It seemed no small coincidence that the opening chapters of *Two Worlds for Memory* tell of the wonderful help and encouragement given to Alfred Noyes by R. C. Lehmann, the father of John Lehmann, whose birth in 1907 is recorded by Noyes, with the added information that he is referring to one 'who, a quarter of a century later, was to be the editor of *New Writing*'!

The television interview with Lord Brockway, referred to in a preceding paragraph, included his recollections of the imprisonment and trial of Roger Casement. How astonished I was to find in Alfred Noyes's autobiography a long chapter describing his own unhappy involvement in the events of those days. The circumstances as related were wholly new to me, given that I grew up in what were then regarded as these 'remote northern isles', and only now in my seventies does my reading enable me to catch up with long past events! One is forced, however, to dwell again on the frightful problems caused by so-called 'patriotism' and 'nationhood'. Is it not time for man to contemplate on higher values than those evoked by either patriotism or nationality? The very survival of our planet depends on how we view this question.

Reading *Two Worlds for Memory* led to yet another coincidence. The opening chapters tell that at the time of writing 'The Highwayman' Alfred Noyes lived in a village 'at the edge of Bagshot Heath'. I asked myself whether this could be near London? The TV news programme a few minutes later, concerning an escape from Broadmoor, showed a map on which Bagshot was pinpointed!

Chapter 13

Religion

> Love from whom the world begun
> Hath the secret of the sun.
> (Robert Bridges, 1844–1930)

'There is no evidence that man was aboriginally endowed with the ennobling belief in the existence of an Omnipotent God. On the contrary there is ample evidence, derived not from hasty travellers, but from men who have long resided with savages, that numerous races have existed, and still exist, who have no idea of one or more gods, and who have no words in their language to express such an idea. The question is, of course, wholly distinct from that higher one, whether there exists a Creator and Ruler of the Universe; and this has been answered in the affirmative by some of the highest intellects that have ever existed.'
(Darwin (1809–1882) writing in *Descent of Man*)

and again

'The feeling of religious devotion is a highly complex one, consisting of love, complete submission to an exalted and mysterious superior, a strong sense of dependence, fear, reverence, gratitude, hope for the future, and perhaps other elements. No being could experience so complex an emotion until advanced in his intellectual and moral faculties to at least a moderately high level. Nevertheless, we see some distant approach to this state of mind in the deep love of a dog for his master, associated with complete submission, some fear, and perhaps other feelings . . . Professor

Branbach goes so far as to maintain that a dog looks on his master as on a god.'

(Ibid.)

The above passages are quoted because they show that Darwin, whose remarkable discoveries in the nineteenth century resulted in wide acceptance of the theory of evolution, was aware of the unique and specialized process by which the mind of man must have evolved until 'some of the highest intellects that have ever existed' were able to express their belief in a creator and ruler of the Universe.

Further, it will be seen that Darwin was aware that true religious devotion is based on love, which, taking precedence over all other emotions, should then dictate all actions. With this awareness it is not surprising to find him saying, in his autobiography, 'My theology is a simple muddle', for theology in the nineteenth century was still confined within rigid doctrines.

It was William Barclay, who, writing about the orthodoxy of Calvinism, observed that its many doctrines failed to mention the love of God as being the main foundation of all belief. On the subject of doctrines and dogma Vagaland had this to say:

> Fruits of misguided science
> are comfortless to me
> And there is little solace
> in cold theology.
> (Nativity Play, 1967)

Crucifixion, surely the most horrific example of man's inhumanity to man, appears to have been a form of execution meted out barbarously in the time of Christ, for we read that some 20,000 rebels were crucified in the Sicilian Slave Rising. Mankind was, then as now, in sore need of divine revelation, and the interpretation of God as a God of Love.

Not very long after his death on the cross, during the missions of Paul and Barnabas, we find Christ's followers holding conflicting views about religious laws and doctrines in their efforts to reconcile their traditional Jewish faith with Christ's teaching. Differences of interpretation of the new Christian faith seem to have continued when the first Christian churches came into being. The first of these was the Eastern Church in the Holy Land (it was later to become the Eastern Orthodox Church, which rejected Papal authority in the ninth or eleventh century A.D.); next was the Church of Rome, which spread quickly through the Roman Empire, with the Pope regarded as successor of St. Peter, and recognized as its supreme authority; then followed other Churches of the East – the Armenian Jacobite, etc., and the Coptic churches; and, at a much later period in history, Protestantism, with its wide variety of denominations and sects, developed from the Reformation in the sixteenth century.

This diversity of churches and doctrines can be seen to be the result of well-intentioned attempts to encapsulate the meaning and mystery of Christ's life, death and resurrection, and it seems that differences have arisen from earliest times because of conflicting, and too literal, interpretations of individual passages of the New Testament, and, in particular, the Gospels.

Despite these differences, it is a sombre thought that the Bible, with its main Christian message of love and forgiveness, might not have been preserved as a legacy for our own generation, had not Christian believers organized themselves in those early and turbulent times into hierarchies of orthodoxy, so that the teachings of the gospels have been preserved down the long centuries when the mass of people could neither read nor write. Translations of the Bible became available in this country only to a limited degree in the sixteenth century when the first printing presses were introduced, and one assumes that the Bible only became fully available for reading by the general public in this country when compulsory education was introduced in 1870.

The survival of the Bible, so widely distributed throughout the world, can be seen as part of a divine plan, but we must bear in mind that the Bible writers were writing for their own times, and none of them, writing individually, could claim to have the whole truth, any more than we, in our own times, have, any of us, a monopoly of the truth. A coincidence a few years ago reminded me that this is so. Before going out one morning, I read in the book which I was about to return to the library (*The Inheritors* by Richard Church) the words:

> Knowledge increases unreality
> The words are Yeats': the certainty is mine
> So far as I have knowledge.

A few hours later I brought home from our local library Kenneth Hopkins' book *English Poetry – a Short History*, and read, in its dedication,

To know all knowledge leaves the truth unknown.

The very first Christians were those of Christ's own generation, his friends and followers, who had listened to his teachings, and seen or experienced his love and compassion, which seemed to have no limits, drawing as it did on an unseen source. It was to these people who had been held close to him by the divine bond of love that he appeared after his cruel death. Their visions of the risen Christ gave them an insight into the full power of God's love, so that life took on a new meaning. These were the people who, along with the disciples, and, later, Paul (whose experience of Christ can only be guessed at – was it a vision as well as a voice?) carried Christ's message to all who would listen. Love, which had overcome death, gave them courage to pass on their message, often to an antagonistic world and even at the cost of suffering and death. They saw the love which was in Christ as the expression of the ultimate goodness against which no evil would ever prevail. The vision has never been lost and finds modern expression in Vagaland's poem 'Vera Crux':

> Wood may be riven and stone be splintered
>   but tyrants cannot kill
> That Tree the tempest shook at Hattin[1] –
>   it lives and blossoms still.
>
> The breath of Spring breathes from it ever,
>   though other growth shall fade;
> No evil thing that shuns the daylight
>   crouches beneath its shade.
>
> There is no ferry at the Jordan,
>   no fee that man can pay;
> But o'er the ford hang starry blossoms
>   lighting the darkened way.

The reference in the first verse to the twelfth-century Crusades is a sad reminder that the symbol of the cross – a cross which was intended to bring peace among mankind – was so misguidedly carried in those far-off religious wars. One feels sure that war has no part in the message of the

---

[1] This line, with its reference to Hattin, was incomplete in the original draft. The wording was suggested by Ernest Marwick and adopted by me in order that the poem might be preserved.

Cross, although, alas, war may follow when its message has been violated (where, for instance, the greed for possessions rides roughshod over the rights of peoples).

In one of his Essays Aldous Huxley wrote: 'Much of the restlessness and uncertainty so characteristic of our time is probably due to the chronic sense of unappeased desires from which men naturally religious, but condemned by circumstances to have no religion, are bound to suffer.' In our own free society it is difficult to see what circumstances could prevent anyone from having a religion, for instance, even a simple belief in the existence of God, but I suspect the reference here was to the difficulty of making a choice among a variety of religions and beliefs and subscribing to their orthodoxies. William Barclay wisely remarked that it needs courage to confound fossilized orthodoxy with living faith.

In the Essay referred to, Aldous Huxley described the various substitutes for religion 'none of which are more than partially adequate'. Among those he mentions are: nationalism, extreme democracy, ritual (he quotes Ku Klux Klan, and even community singing!), sex (which dominates modern minds to the point of obsession – my words), business or commerce, and lastly, the arts, comprising literature, painting, poetry, etc.

I notice that Hans Kung includes technology and capitalism among the surrogates. In present times perhaps sport should also be added?

There are, indeed, writers today who are putting forward the idea that art may fill the gap where religion and philosophy have failed. It must be conceded that in the past some of the greatest works of art have been inspired by religion. But according to Richard Hoggart (Open University programme, 24.7.83), 'not poetry, not art . . . loving one's neighbour as oneself is the serious thing' was the conclusion reached by W. H. Auden.

Reference to the arts as a substitute for religion brings to mind an occasion when I had to consider this concept. In church, one Sunday in October 1975, I listened to an exposition on the fourteenth chapter of Hosea, in which the speaker indicated the danger of even an artistic gift becoming an idol to be worshipped. I immediately thought, 'Surely Alex's (my husband's) poetry could not be regarded in this light' and was reassured by the further thought that his poetry was mainly a vehicle for his own religious convictions. My note made on the following day, 27th October 1975, reads: 'I recently bought Aldous Huxley's *Point Counter Point*, which I am reading with great difficulty, and often distaste, because of the cynical outlook of some of the characters. To my astonishment I find one of them – Burlap – saying, concerning the French poet Rimbaud:

"Oh! To be the finest poet of your generation, and knowing it, to give up poetry – that's losing your life to save it . . ."'!

My widest reading has been done since my husband's death in 1973. I cannot say now which I read first, the Essay or the novel (*Point Counter Point*), but it is interesting to discover that in both the idea of the 'artistic surrogate' was being pursued by Huxley.

Belief in God, or a supreme power, is surely the basis of all true religion, and, whether admitted or not, instinctive recognition of this power seems to lie deep within the consciousness of the human race. In a radio broadcast report about the Fastnet sailing tragedy in September 1979, in which the sea claimed so many lives, one of the competitors interviewed said that he had never before in his life prayed, but that this was a time when he did.

In *Life and Letters* Thomas Huxley (1825–1895), grandfather of Julian and Aldous, wrote: 'Of all the senseless babble I have ever had occasion to read, the demonstrations of the philosophers who undertake to tell us about the nature of God would be the worst if they were not surpassed by the still greater absurdities of the philosophers who try to prove there is no God.'

While on radio we hear that most scientists and theologians seem now to be in agreement about the 'big bang' theory of the 'origin' of the universe, the question still remains: what existed before the 'big bang'?

Notice the use of the word 'origin' instead of the word 'creation'. It is interesting that most writers, atheist and agnostic alike, of books about the evolution of plants, lower and higher animals, including man, use the words 'creation', implying a creator, 'design', implying a designer, 'plan', implying a planner, and so on.

As remarked also on radio, a vocabulary for 'unbelievers' has not yet been arrived at. However, attempts are occasionally made to overcome this problem, as in *The Sky at Night* programme, which (3.5.81) spoke of 'The Way the Universe was Born'. But can anything be born out of nothing?

Einstein is said to have remarked: 'What really interests me is whether God had any choice in the creation of the world!' One could wish that he had enlarged upon this cryptic remark. He is also said to have remarked that 'God and nature do not play at dice', which I take to mean that the laws of the physical universe are immutable, that is, once created they cannot be changed.

A verse from Vagaland's dialect poem '*L'Anse aux Meadows*' puts the case unequivocally:

Whin the folk apo dis planet starts ta winder what's aroond dem
Dan der wan thing shöre – o dat I hae nae doot;
Nae maitter foo dey sheeks an spaek an traep wi een anidder,
Foo hit aa began dey never will fin oot;
Whaar hit cam fae, dat dey never will fin oot.

I cannot resist making the following 'Irish' observation: if any man, in his search for an explanation of the origin of the universe, were to achieve the impossible and discover it, would he not expect to receive due acknowledgement?

From the word 'agnosticism' – coined by Professor Huxley in 1869 (from the word in Acts XVII where St. Paul challenged the Athenians for raising an altar 'to the unknown God') – comes 'agnostic' meaning '(adherent) of the view that nothing is known or likely to be known of the existence of God or of anything beyond material phenomena' (*Concise Oxford Dictionary*).

But Paul undoubtedly had a mystical experience (non-material and of a kind not verifiable by science) which persuaded him of the purpose and meaning of Christ's mission on earth. It is, I believe, generally held that Paul would not have known Jesus in the latter's life on earth, but is this an established fact? If so, it is all the more remarkable that Paul's subsequent testimony seems to have outstripped in zeal that of the disciples and other followers of Christ. The records of his journeyings by land and sea through most of the Mediterranean area are impressive evidence of the hardships he was prepared to undergo in the cause of his new-found faith.

Mystical experiences are not, however, confined to those related in the Bible. If it were so, it is doubtful whether the Christian message would have survived. Its survival is in great measure due to the witness of Christian saints and martyrs throughout the centuries down to the present day, not forgetting poets and religious writers. A faith which has been handed down at great cost is not something to be cast lightly aside.

How do we see Christ in our own day and age? Frances Young's contribution to *The Myth of God Incarnate* has these words with which the question should, I think, be approached:

'It is not by accepting traditional formulations as God-given and unquestionable that we join the band of witnesses in the New Testament and the early church, but by wrestling with the prob-

---

shöre – sure; sheeks – talk excessively; traep – argue.

lem of expressing intelligently in our own contemporary environment our personal testimony to the redemptive effect of faith in Jesus of Nazareth.'

and, borrowing from the words of Maurice Wiles in the same book, I am content to say that I see Christ as one who embodies a full and unique response of man to God, and, at the same time, as one who embodies the way of God to men – in other words, in Christ we see the effect of a perfect relationship with God, and the fulfilment of that love required by the two commandments 'on which hang all the law and the prophets'.

As Bamber Gascoigne remarked in his book *The Christians*, 'Christianity has made a habit of surviving'. And why? Because the spirit of God which was in Christ has been handed down, generation by generation, through the most faithful of His followers, His saints and martyrs. Have we not seen examples in our own day?

At this point in my writing I 'took a break', and, after making a cup of tea, turned on the radio to listen, as I thought, to the programme *Bookshelf*, but I had mistaken the day and time of Frank Delaney's talk. To my surprise I heard a discussion about 'one of the major religious thinkers of the twentieth century – Charles Raven', whose name was completely new to me.[2] Much of what was being said about his approach to Christianity seemed to support some of the views I have been trying to express.

Among writers who have been described either as 'atheist' or 'agnostic' is Thomas Hardy. From writing novels he turned in later life to poetry. The term 'sardonic' has sometimes been applied to his lyrics, but does not the following poem, at least, reveal an awareness that the power of love rules in realms seen and unseen?

> My spirit will not haunt the mound
>   Above my breast,
> But travel, memory-possessed,
> To where my tremulous being found
>   Life largest, best.
>
> My phantom-footed shape will go
>   When nightfall grays
> Hither and thither along the ways

---

[2] Canon Charles Raven is, however, mentioned in Vera Brittain's book, *Testament of Experience* which I read some years later, in 1983.

> I and another used to know
> In backward days.
>
> And there you'll find me, if a jot
> You still should care
> For me, and for my curious air;
> If otherwise, then I shall not,
> For you, be there.

I discovered this poem only a few years ago. Previously I had not been familiar with Hardy's poetry, and had read only some of his novels. I have a vivid recollection of his novels *Under the Greenwood Tree* and *Far From the Madding Crowd* which we read in class at school, and whose descriptions of life in the Wessex countryside of those days gave one the feeling of being a part of it.

Hardy's writing seems to have appealed to other people for the same reason. In a review of Vagaland's poetry in *Scotland's Magazine*, April 1966, A. D. Mackie told how he had been reading 'along with T. A. Robertson' (Vagaland) . . . 'a totally different poet, Dylan Thomas. . . . Both were writing about the places they loved, and each in his own way conveyed the very breath of the places he was writing about.' And he went on to say: 'You become conscious of the Thomas countryside, just as you become an inhabitant of Thomas Hardy's Wessex, without ever having to be in the place.'

That Hardy was agnostic rather than atheist in the latter part of his life was made clear in 'Apology', which introduced his *Late Lyrics and Earlier*. Here he showed his concern about the dogmatic stand maintained by the Church, with consequent loss of opportunity of 'gathering of many millions of waiting agnostics into its fold'. . . . And he asked: 'What other purely English establishment than the Church . . . is left in this country to keep the shreds of morality together?'

In the same paragraph Hardy spoke of evidence, at least in some parts of the English Church, of '"Removing those things that are shaken", in accordance with the wise epistolary recommendations to the Hebrews.'

This trend of thought finds full expression in the last chapter of *The Lion's Mouth*, the autobiography of our modern poet, Kathleen Raine. She writes:

> 'If I am to be true to what I imaginatively perceive, I must say that it is of no use to try to keep the leaves from falling, green

though they once were, and lament as we must their fading. The nihilists would agree; but they desire the death of the tree, the dismantling of civilization, nor do they believe in those divine originals Christendom has embodied and reflected. Yet it is not those leaves which cling longest against the wind of change that are obedient to the tree's life, but the seed cast adrift, the end as it is the beginning of the life cycle. The great tree is at this time showering down its leaves in a process of death which cannot be arrested, and whose record is everywhere to be read in the nihilism of the arts, of social life, in a thousand images of disintegration, in the reversion of civilized society, it may be, to a state of barbarism.

'The mustard-seed (smallest of all seeds) is a symbol of the dimensionless point through which the timeless interior order ("the Kingdom of Heaven is within") issues into the time-process, and returns again into the inner world. From the seed the tree grows; as Rome from the apostolic, Byzantium from a marriage of the Greek and the patriarchal vision. What is latent in the seminal vision is, in the process of time, projected into the thousand arts and *mores* of a civilization; or of an individual life-time. But when the process has been completed, when all that was latent in that seed has been made manifest, is there not then a reversal, an inbreathing, a withdrawal, as the psychologists would put it, of those projections which, reflecting and embodying themselves, were the agents of civilization? . . .

'Those who are indissolubly wedded to the external forms, whether of a religion or of a culture, must at this time despair; unable to withdraw from these what for centuries has been projected into them, they lose, when these fail, portions of their souls; but those who are able to rediscover within themselves all that has been progressively withdrawn from our dismantled world, need not fear the withdrawal of the informing presence from the beautiful forms itself created.

'The process of death cannot be arrested, civilizations cannot be saved; but there are the seeds, the living among the dead, who do not participate in the collective disintegration, but guard their secret of immortality, the essence of what has been and may be again. Who can say into what soil these seeds may be sown, or into what region of the universe the harvest of the world is gathered?'

Notice the similarity of thought: Thomas Hardy – 'removing those things that are shaken'. Kathleen Raine – 'it is of no use to try to keep the leaves from falling'. What other hope can we have than that the 'divine originals', which the best of Christendom has embodied and reflected through 2,000 years, will continue to be preserved by 'seeds cast adrift'?

Chapter 14

Poetry and Religion

Hardy's hope, 'a mere dream, perhaps', was of 'an alliance between religion, which must be retained unless the world is to perish, and complete rationality, which must come, unless also the world is to perish, by means of the interfusing effect of poetry.'

In the December 1976 number of *Books and Bookmen*, Konstantin Bazarov expressed the view that religion is 'neurosis in the full sense, the means through which mankind during most of his history has avoided the challenge of taking responsibility for his own emotional life', and, wishing apparently to state this challenge in poetical terms, he quoted these lines from Thomas Hardy's poem 'A Plaint to Man':

> When you slowly emerged from the den of Time,
> And gained percipience as you grew,
> And fleshed you fair out of shapeless slime,
> Wherefore, O Man did there come to you
> The unhappy need of creating me –
> A form like your own – for praying to?
> ....
> ....
> The truth should be told, and the fact be faced
> That had best been faced in earlier years:
> The fact of life with dependence placed
> On the human heart's resource alone
> And visioned help unsought, unknown.

The poem, I see, was written between the years 1909 and 1910, when Hardy, it seems, was already retreating into a position of agnosticism, for reasons which were later explained in 'Apology' – his introduction to the *Late Lyrics and Earlier* – but it is interesting to find that there are two lines missing from those quoted by Bazarov. The poem, in fact, concludes thus:

> The truth should be told, and the fact be faced
> That had best been faced in earlier years:
>
> The fact of life with dependence placed
> On the human heart's resource alone,
> *In brotherhood bonded close and graced*
> *With loving-kindness fully blown*[1]
> And visioned help unsought, unknown.

Ouspensky, according to Fritz Peters, called love 'the most powerful of all emotions', and love is being invoked by Hardy in the two lines which were omitted by Bazarov. Here, unwittingly, it seems, Hardy introduced the interfusing effect of poetry as the alliance between religion and rationality. 'Loving-kindness fully-blown', as I see it, can emanate from none other than God, on whom, as Father, the brotherhood of man depends.

Agnosticism is said to be 'the view that nothing is known or likely to be known of the existence of God, or of anything beyond material phenomena' (*Concise Oxford Dictionary*). Is loving-kindness a material phenomenon?

No one would deny that the various religions down the ages have, sadly, often been 'characterised by intolerant fanaticism and dogmatism' as Konstantin Bazarov rightly pointed out, and wherever this happened the masses were following blindly leaders who, so far as Christianity was involved, themselves either missed the whole meaning of Christ's message or chose to ignore it in their greed for power.

It was Shelley, I believe, who wrote that poets are the unacknowledged legislators of the world. Shelley's dictum must, I believe, include those poets whose words have been used in Christian worship throughout the centuries, and up to the present day. Many of the hymns we now hear sung on Sunday evenings, on radio and television programmes, have words inspired by our best loved poets, some written as long ago as the twelfth

---

[1] my italics.

(St. Bernard of Clairvaux), thirteenth (St. Francis of Assisi) and seventeenth (John Bunyan and John Milton) centuries.

Nearer modern times we are sustained by hymns such as 'Lead, Kindly Light' (words by John Henry Newman), 'There is a Land of Pure Delight' and 'When I survey the Wondrous Cross' (Isaac Watts), 'Abide with Me' (Henry Francis Lyte). The last-mentioned used to be sung regularly by crowds at football matches but it seems to have been replaced by chants with words having little meaning ('Here we go, here we go') or by nationalistic songs which can tend to denigrate our common humanity.

It must be some fifteen to twenty years since the idea of recording 'coincidences', some of which were later to be included in this book, occurred to me. The MS. which resulted grew to unexpected proportions and was abandoned for some years because of bereavements; then submitted to, but not accepted by, two publishers, one in England, one in Scotland. However, these did not seem to be outright rejections, and I have recently been making a few alterations, one of which has been to divide the original chapter on 'Religion' into two, the second being headed 'Poetry and Religion'. I had proceeded to write about the inspirational words of many of our hymns when, *the same evening*, in the *Songs of Praise* programme, I heard the Rev. Colin Morris making a spirited exposition of the benefit to be derived from the community singing of hymns, the words of which are a precious legacy, familiar to, and treasured by, those taking part, and also the listening public, among all of whom there may be many who are no longer churchgoers.

Poetry which reveals a search for faith also seems to have relevance here. When I edited my husband's poems in 1975 our friend, Ernest Marwick in Orkney, suggested that the poem 'Shiplack' should be followed by 'Bound is the Boatless Man'.

'Shiplack' appeared in *Laeves fae Vagaland*, the first collection of his poems published in 1952:

> Around the island, surging,
>   Are countless leagues of sea
> Where I can travel, urging,
>   Far out, my horse of tree.
>
> Freed from the sooty rafter
>   My body, yet no goal,
> That I can follow after,
>   For ship-lack of the soul.

To voyage where stars are reeling
    Man needs another keel
Than wood, where sap of feeling
    Still runs, from Yggdrasil.

None enters Eden's portal –
    Its trees are fenced by flame;
And who but saints immortal
    Can seek the Tree of Shame?

Yet thoughts are still recorded
    As man now hopes, now grieves;
We walk where, many-worded,
    Thick float the drifting leaves.

However, a sense of purpose and hope for the human situation has been arrived at in 'Bound is the Boatless Man', which was included in *Mair Laeves* published in 1965 and which takes its title from a Faeroese proverb.

When evil power unfettered,
    A gale of hate and strife,
Has swept the outer ocean
    Bare of all human life,

We scan the dim horizon,
    Where still the storm-clouds lour,
For spars and planks of driftwood
    The seas may not devour:

Wreckage of worthy vessels
    That proudly tacked or ran –
The Liberty, The Comrade,
The Brotherhood of Man –

Launched by the men before us
    who sought for others' good;
And now, of all their efforts,
    Only some sea-scarred wood.

Fragments of battered timber –
Teak, larch, enduring oak –
But from them may be fashioned
Keel, 'hassen', 'routh' and stroke.

A homely vessel, maybe,
We build as best we can,
To take us out of bondage:
'Bound is the boatless man.'

And when in storms we founder
We, too, may leave behind
Some broken bits of flotsam
For other men to find.

Both these poems view life as a voyage over a boundless sea. It is hardly surprising that the influence of the sea surrounding Shetland's islands (the sea is said to be never more than three miles distant from any point on the land) should feature so regularly in Vagaland's poetry. In 'Alamootie', for instance, man's situation is compared to that of the young storm petrels setting out on their first flight over the Western ocean:

Sae wi man – he lives a saison
Apo da aidge o a boondless sea.

Darwin said that there was 'no evidence that man was originally endowed with the ennobling belief in the existence of an omnipotent God', but we do know that from earliest times man lived in fear and dread of elements over which he had no control but which he hoped might in some way be appeased, and these elements gradually took shape in his mind as gods to be worshipped. How then did it come about that the god or gods who had inspired only fear and dread came to be recognized as one omnipotent god, whose chief attribute was love, which bound God to man, man to God, and man to man? The first of the ten commandments given by Moses in the Old Testament tells in unequivocal words that man in this further stage of his intellectual evolution had begun to discern the omnipotent power of Love.

---

hassen – board; routh – wood protecting the gunwale of a boat.

One cannot help speculating that the Omnipotent Mind behind the creation of the universe had in view the evolution of man to the stage when he could recognize that his ability to distinguish between good and evil depended wholly on, and was in proportion to, his love of God and his love for his fellow man. Only when man has progressed to a full understanding of the power of love will he be able to exercise wisely his freedom to choose between good and evil. In the wide field of science, research, technology, medicine, etc., this must mean giving due consideration to the possible effects of man's intervention with the physical laws of the universe.

The universe is of necessity governed by certain relentless physical laws whose operation sometimes results in natural disasters which man finds difficult to reconcile with the idea of a loving God, and, yet, without these laws it seems obvious that chaos would result. They are laws which cannot be interrupted to accommodate man. In 'Above Scafell' Vagaland voices thoughts which occurred to him during a night journey by air over the peaks of Cumbria, at a time when he was recovering from a serious operation:

> Above Scafell, we watch the peaks upthrusting
>   beneath the outspread wing,
> And trust the crew to bear us o'er the ridges
>   where snow can hardly cling.
>
> Below us glimmering white and rocky darkness,
>   gateways to death are near.
> The plane goes on – whatever ills o'ertake us
>   there is no landfall here.
>
> And so it is with man, who through the skyway
>   speeds from his hour of birth,
> Yet knows not all the perils of the darkness
>   around the spinning earth.
>
> Men ask for help, and, if there is no answer,
>   are all their prayers in vain?
> The guardian angels cannot wreck a planet
>   to save a soul from pain.

In his last illness my husband's calm courage, and concern for others, were evidence of the strength of the convictions which had so often been expressed in his poetry. Many of his poems had an unequivocal moral ending – what, I suppose, Nabokov would have called a *'pointe assassine'* – but it was contrary to his nature to do other than state the truth as he saw it. In other words, 'tell the vision, and write it plain'. Unlike so many modern writers, he did not often reveal the intimate wrestlings of his soul. Instead he preferred to delay until he could state clearly the conclusions he had arrived at.

My note made on 1st May 1975 reads: 'With the radio switched on for the 1.00 p.m. news and the comments which follow in *The World at One*, I allowed my thoughts to wander, and found myself having an imaginary interview about Alex and his poetry in which I said that he believed in the "power of God".' Immediately following this, there came over the radio the words '. . . is no longer the power of God'. I was able to recapture the beginning of the sentence (the mind's facility for doing this is remarkable). The discussion had been about Vietnam, and the interviewee had said that, 'America could no longer regard herself as the power of God!'

Patrick MacGill, the 'navvy poet' I have referred to elsewhere, in his poem 'Heroes' has thoughts about the power of God, as expressed in the unrelenting physical laws of the universe:

May Heaven pity the sailor-man when the Northern doom's abroad,
For the ship is built by the human hand, the berg by the hand of God.

A serious breakdown in my health in 1952 was brought about to a large extent by overwork, but the deep underlying cause was unresolved inner conflict. This unwillingness, or inability, to face squarely problems which disturb one's inner peace no doubt accounts for the wide prevalence of mental breakdowns in modern society. The words of Polonius to his son, 'This above all, to thine own self be true' are evidence that in Shakespeare's day also the dangers of inner conflict were fully recognized. And so it must have been from the earliest dawning in man's consciousness of a distinction between good and evil. We seem to be living in an age which tries to deny this distinction, with the resultant suppression of moral standards. Can we afford to ignore the lessons so painfully learned by past civilizations?

When interviewed by Bernard Levin on television Dr. Jonas Salk expressed the view that the potential for all that has emerged in the course of evolution must have pre-existed. (*The Listener*, 17.6.82.) This seems a reasonable conclusion, and yet the scientific discoveries of the last century or more, and the theory of evolution now widely accepted, have had the unfortunate and illogical result of aggrandising man's faith in himself, seeing himself, ultimately, as 'dictator of the universe', no longer depending on a superior source of strength. In *The Perennial Philosophy* Aldous Huxley quoted these words of Werner Heisenberg, the physicist: 'For the first time in history man on this planet is discovering that he is alone with himself, without a partner, and without an adversary.' And I believe it was Julian Huxley who wrote a book entitled *Man Stands Alone*. However, in the concluding paragraphs of his autobiography *Memories II*, written towards the end of a long life, Julian Huxley seems to have become increasingly aware of the perilous road along which humanity is travelling in its haste to create an improved social order. In summing up, he comments on the replacement of traditional morality by permissiveness, 'with its different rules and limitations', 'the deep sense of insecurity which prevails all over our planet, leading to hatred and violence', and he goes on to express doubts about the rapid advances in scientifically based technology, sometimes applied with disastrous consequences. His final appeal is to 'man's reason, natural intelligence and conscience'.

But by what means is man to preserve, and acknowledge, the demands of his 'conscience'? For, while his intellectual skill and ingenuity can be said to have evolved to an astonishing degree, increasing his ability to exploit the fabric of the universe, can the same be said of his conscience, suppression of which may so easily result from failure to draw on his only source of enlightenment – his God of Love?

That God has final control of his universe is the view expressed in Vagaland's dialect poem 'Michael':

> Ee day ida heicht o Simmer
> whin da sun wis baetin doon,
> We göd trowe da grinnd o a gairden
> at wis far fae ony toon.
>
> Dey wirna a soond ta be heard dere
> bit da dronn o da drummie-bees,
> As we waandered roond ida stillness
> ta look at da flooers an trees.

---

göd trowe da grinnd – went through the gate; toon – town.

An we saa in a shaltered coarner,
   wi da laeves abön his head,
Da statue o a Angel
   in aa his airmer cled.

He stöd, wi his graet wings faaldit,
   whaar da laeves wis growin green,
An he linned him apo da haandle
   o a swird at wis lang an keen.

Half waaken he seemed, half draemin,
   sae calm wis his face o sten;
An he didna seem ta be leetin
   da wyes an da warks o men.

Bit in ida paece o da gairden,
   ida scentit Simmer air,
I lookit at da Angel
   an wis blyde ta see him dere.

Fir men can shut a rocket
   ta laand apo da Mön;
Dey can send dir space-craft vaigin
   among da starns abön.

Da Eart wi what dey're inventit
   is maybe a better place,
Bit some o dem never learns
   da wye ta live in paece.

Da pör wild baests is huntit
   whaarever dey shance ta be,
An canna wirt fin shalter
   at da aidge o da Arctic Sea.

---

swird – sword; shut – shoot; canna wirt – cannot even.

Some men maan aye be tapsters
an aa at dey want dey tak,
Nae maitter what sowls dey hatter,
nae maitter what herts dey brak.

Dey could drap wan bomb, an a ceety
wid geng up in a glöd o flame,
Bit I wat at Göd's airmy o angels
is michtier still as dem.

---

tapster – 'boss'.

Chapter 15

The Mysterious World of Thought

> When we are growing old and deepening shadows
> Blot out the path where we have wandered far,
> When we know not the place to which we journey
> Unlit by moon or star;
> The thoughts of others who have truly loved us
> May flow towards us on the channelled air,
> Guiding us to a place beyond the darkness
> To find a garden there.
> (from 'Night-scented Stock' by Vagaland)

Thoughts – where do they come from? Nearly forty years ago, when I was recovering from the breakdown already mentioned, I had an experience which caused me to wonder briefly about the strange world of thought. On one of the solitary walks which I frequently took in the neighbouring countryside, I had the peculiar sensation of a thought 'landing' on my consciousness, as though on a receiving set of some kind. Neurologists may have an explanation for this occurrence? A colleague at work had told me in the early stages of my illness that I was 'like a piece of elastic that had been stretched too far'. Was there, during my gradual recovery, a sudden uniting or healing of nerve strands which caused the entry of thought to 'register'?

Most people would agree that thoughts are given to us with the power to accept or reject them, and it seems to me that we are surrounded by forces, a heterogeneous mixture of good and evil, which strive to influence us in different directions. I think we must accept that there are *evil* forces, evident enough in misguided humanity, but where do they originate? John Hick, writing in *Death and Eternal Life*, refers to 'the traditional catholic idea that the moral quality of each individual life, when completed, influences this world'. This could mean that each individual at his death has made a contribution to the influences for good or evil which surround us.

How else can we view man's behaviour at this stage in his so-called evolution, his ingenuity being used so often for the destruction of mankind rather than its preservation? Compared with behaviour in the animal world from which it is contended he has evolved, man's record of behaviour, resulting solely from his greed for wealth and power, is appalling. In *On the Shores of Endless Worlds*, by Andrew Tomas, we read that 'man is the only creature on earth that destroys his own species on a mass scale. In the armed conflicts of the twentieth century 36 million civilians and 27 million military personnel were killed. The number of wounded, incapacitated and psychologically dislocated was many times greater.' In the same book the author tells us: 'The world stockpile of nuclear weapons is now equivalent to 10 tons of TNT per head of earth's population, whereas only a few grammes are needed to kill one individual.' If that was indeed the position in 1974, when the book was published, what are the subsequent increases in the world's stockpile – held presumably by the major world powers – supposed to achieve, short of the complete destruction of Planet Earth?

If it is the moral quality of our life which survives when we die, it seems clear that there must be a final reckoning, not necessarily here on earth, but, possibly, ultimately in the spiritual universe. St. Paul (Acts 24: 15) reminded his accusers that he believed, with them, that there was to be a resurrection of good and wicked alike.

Teilhard de Chardin believed that there is a continuous layer of thought around the earth. It seems to me that ideas do come from the thought world surrounding us, and, if so, man's intellectual evolution does not depend solely on genetic make-up and environment.

How far can any human being assume personal credit for 'bright ideas'? It does, of course, take an alert mind to assess their value. Arthur Koestler, in his book *The Ghost in the Machine*, when referring to scientific discoveries and the events or situations which trigger them off, remarks that if the chance event which is reported to have led to a particular discovery had not occurred, some other event would have acted similarly on the prepared mind, or some other contemporary mind. As Magnus Pyke points out in his book *There and Back*, a discovery is hardly ever the result of a series of rationally linked intellectual steps.

It is questionable, therefore, whether man should be assuming to himself credit for thoughts which are given to him, simply because he has been blessed with a good 'brain', part of which serves him as a good 'receiving set' if he is properly 'tuned in'. Great thinkers, including scientists, have to be open to ideas, and many a person who has had a 'bright idea' would be the first to admit to not knowing whence it came![1] It was refreshing to hear Eric Laithwaite, Professor of Heavy Electrical Engineering at Imperial College, London, say on radio some years ago that there were times when he felt he got ideas 'from somewhere else'. His further comment that 'we could destroy ninety-nine per cent of the human race, but there would be a few thousand crawl out of the holes at the end' brought to mind this verse from Vagaland's 'October Poppy':

> An noo da wirld is nearly shakken sindry
> An nae man kyins what he might live ta see.
> An yet I tink whin war an strife is endit
> Apo Göd's Eart, dey'll still be some-een dere
> Ta look apo da laeks o dee, bricht poppy,
>   An tink da sicht is fair.

Some recent writing suggests that thoughts and ideas arise from 'an unconscious' – in each individual person, I suppose. This could mean that our so-called 'unconscious' is simply the *route* by which thought, with its potential for good or ill, reaches individual consciousness. What is generally described as 'telepathy', implying transference of thought from one person to another, comes into question here. Tolstoy spoke of 'the instinctive feeling with which one human being guesses another's thoughts'. My own experiences seem to point rather to thought, from an outer source or sources, being directed to two minds at the same time. A lifelong friend and I, who worked in the same office in London years ago, repeatedly found ourselves having the same thought, or uttering the same words together, at the same time. To mark the occasion, it was our custom, before saying another word, to link fingers and name a favourite

---

[1] I find that Rider Haggard wrote in his Journal on 22nd May 1918 that in a conversation with Kipling the latter commented that 'anything any of us did *well* was no credit to us: that it came from somewhere else; "We are only telephone wires"'. (The Penguin *Concise Dictionary of Biographical Quotation* – ed. Justin Wintle and Richard Kevin.)

And, in an Open University programme concerning experimental science which I chanced upon as recently as February 1983, it was said of Locke, who along with Bacon and Newton had contributed so much to modern science, that his ideas came to him 'through the senses'.

---

shakken sindry – shaken asunder; dey'll – there will.

poet. I have no idea where this ritual practice originated – it was accepted by us without question! But it did seem appropriate that the mystery of the occasion should be 'blessed' in some way.

In *Astride the Two Cultures*, W. H. Thorpe remarks: 'The origin of consciousness is as mysterious as the origin of life itself.' In the same book he quotes these words of Alan Fisher: 'Scientists studying brain function from the inside simply haven't even approached the stage at which the investigation of complex thought processes is either reasonable or possible.' And although optimism for success in this field appears to have been expressed by Professor Daniel Dennett, on Radio 3, in March 1982, when interviewed about his book *The Mind's 'I'*, it seems evident that the 'unforeseen miracle – the emergence of consciousness' which 'differentiates us decisively and permanently from machines' (Gordon Rattray Taylor writing in *The Natural History of the Mind*) will always prove to be the obstacle to any serious investigation.

Chapter 16

Civilization and Ethics

'If any age lacks the minds which force it to reflect about the ethical, the level of its morality sinks, and, with it, its capacity for answering the questions which present themselves.'
(Albert Schweitzer in *Civilization and Ethics*)

On the same day as I had gathered together some notes on genetic engineering, the 1st of April 1980, the TV programme *Nationwide* 'disclosed' what purported to be evidence of horrifying experiments in genetic engineering taking place in a research establishment somewhere in England. The events presented were an illusion, created, in very bad taste, I thought, for 'April Fool's Day'. Genetic engineering and organ transplant operations are subjects with such serious implications that no human being should be prepared to treat them lightly. Did one hear correctly, on a television programme, from the lips of Dr. Barnard himself, that latest heart transplant surgery had used skills gained through providing a dog with two heads?

On the following day, 2nd April, while still thinking about the direction in which man's search for knowledge is taking him, it occurred to me, on my solitary way home from shopping, that, however symbolic the bible story of Adam and Eve may be, it does aim to mark the first dawning in man's consciousness of the distinction between good and evil.

A week or so previously, I had ordered, through our local bookseller, R. C. Scriven's *Edge of Darkness, Edge of Light*. It arrived at the bookseller's on 2nd April, and I brought it home along with my shopping. The first sentence of the book, which I opened shortly afterwards, reads: 'Adam fell for an apple'!

Also on my way home on that same morning I thought about my early childhood in the country before I attended school in Lerwick. I had –

unquestioningly, it seems now – been a willing farm hand, milked cows, and 'mucked out' the byre! 'This is something' – I said to myself – 'which may be worth mentioning in my book.'

Because of the extraordinary coincidence, related at the beginning of this book, connected with R. C. Scriven's radio play, *And a Measure of Sliding Sand*, I read through his autobiography, *Edge of Darkness* . . . almost at one sitting! I learned that he had been orphaned at the age of nine, had been billeted on a farm in Yorkshire, and that one of the first tasks allotted to him had been the 'muckin out' of the byre!

The mystic experience described by Scriven in the latter part of his book has a further strange bearing on these 'coincidences'. His account ends with these words: 'In the nearest thing on earth to the garden of Eden, that is to say, childhood, I had become aware of the tree of the knowledge of good and of evil. In Riffa Wood, I believe I touched the tree God forbade Adam to touch – the tree of life.'

But the series of 'coincidences' does not end there. On 3rd April, the early morning prescribed reading in my Prayer Handbook was Genesis Chapter 3, verses 1–13!

In June 1980, immediately after typing the foregoing from my notes – while searching on behalf of a friend for the date of one of my husband's poems – I discovered by chance, in the Autumn 1956 number of *The New Shetlander* this poem by Ernest Marwick of Orkney, who was later to give me so much help and encouragement with the editing of my husband's poems:

The Apple

Confound this Age, whose greatest art
Is to find the irreducible part,
Deep in the atom's heart to pry
And teach the electrons to deny
Their principle of secret growth –
Creator and consumer both.

Dark powers that long in sleep have lain
Would make creation groan again,
Would rend the rocks and churn the seas,
To bloody mire, and bid the trees
Unleaf, the cities sink in slime,
And make all void a second time.

Was this dark drama played before?
Did we come through this self-same door?
Did we some million years ago
Profane the mysteries, and so,
With knowledge stronger than our will
Make earth a seething crucible?

And did it later come to pass
That, from a cloud of viscid gas,
Another labouring world began,
Compact of waters, rock and man;
Made of the dust, but burdened yet
With secrets dust cannot forget?

Our warning symbol warns no more,
We shall probe Eden's apple to the core;
But at the core such knowledge lies
That he who meddles with it dies –
Here in our midst the tree of knowledge stands;
We have the atom-apple in our hands.

Ernest Marwick (who, owing to ill-health left school at the age of ten) had an outstanding career as writer, journalist and broadcaster, and is remembered as 'Orkney's most distinguished scholar'. His books include *An Anthology of Orkney Verse*, *Orkney Folklore and Traditions*, and *The Folklore of Orkney and Shetland*, the last-mentioned being published in 1975. He was made an honorary burgess of the City and Royal Burgh of Kirkwall in 1975, and in 1976 the honorary degree of Master of Arts was conferred on him by Edinburgh University. He died tragically in a motoring accident in July 1977.

The approaching clouds of darkness so prophetically forecast in Ernest Marwick's poem, published in *The New Shetlander* in 1956, present an even more imminent threat to the world at the present day. But I believe, with a faith which my husband and I shared together, that whatever may be the fate of our world as it at present exists, goodness and innocence will ultimately prevail, and so I introduce here his poem 'Klokkaburn',[1] with its reference to the Garden of Eden:

---

[1] Klokkaburn (Nor. 'klokke' – bell) could, I think, be translated 'tinkling water'.

Da white lamb stöd at his midder's side
doon ower at da burn broo,
An ower his head da white cloods spread
across da Heevin's blue.

Da glansin water ran doon by,
plat-calm da shudden lay,
An his hert wis licht, fir da sun wis bricht
an he could rin an play.

He kyentna at, whin Winter comes,
da Eart wi frost is bund;
Da winds dey blaa, an da moorin snaa
shön covers aa da grund.

Ta him da Eart wis jöst as fair
as whin shö first wis med,
Whin Adam stöd wi da sun-gold's glöd
laek a glory roond his head.

Wi birds an baests aside him dere
athin da gairden green,
An her, da hert o his inner hert,
an da licht o his twa een.

Bit noo da Eart is gettin aald,
an Age comes no alane,
Bit brings his share o döle an care
in ida lives o men.

Yet, whin I see da peerie lambs
playing dem ida Voar,
Da Eart is as bricht ida moarnin-licht
as ever shö wis afore.

Some of the horrors of factory farming were disclosed in a television programme (B.B.C. 2) on 21st October 1982, when one speaker men-

---

glansin – sparkling; shudden – small reedy loch; kyentna – did not know; moorin snaa – drifting snow; shö – she; glöd – glow; hert – heart; döle – grief; in ida – into the.

tioned that lambs might in future be subjected to this form of food production. I suggest that the poem 'Klokkaburn' should give rise to second thoughts about this.

If evolution is regarded as a fact, where is man's compassion for the rest of the animal world which has evolved more slowly than himself? I believe it was St. Thomas Aquinas who wrote: 'It is evident that if a man practises a compassionate affection for animals, he is all the more disposed to feel compassion for his fellowmen.' And, writing in *The Listener* (18th May 1978) D. J. Enright quoted Lewis Carroll as having said that scientists spoke of man as being 'twin brother to the monkey' but when it suited their purpose they argued that 'human and animal suffering differ *in kind*.'

On 6th February 1975, in a local restaurant, a friend and I discussed cancer research, which I was told by my friend was to benefit from the proceeds of the sale of a large house in town. I said I had misgivings about contributing to this research because I was strongly opposed to vivisection and experiments on dumb animals. My contributions go rather to relief of suffering and pain. After this conversation I arrived home and switched on the radio to the programme *The World at One*. To my astonishment a description was being given of an experiment alleged to have been carried out on a dog, a beagle, which was made to smoke in order to find out the effects on the animal's lungs. The animal was said to have suffered, and must have done so.

Protests are made from time to time about the conditions under which animals are transported to Europe for slaughter, and, not surprisingly, protests are increasingly being made about experiments on animals. It seems hardly credible, but, according to my notes, an experiment was described some time ago, on B.B.C. 2, in which a calf was having its heart removed, to be replaced by an artificial one.[2]

Transplant surgery now proceeds relentlessly. How does one describe a civilization which permits the chasing of the (possibly) dying for parts to preserve the living? On one occasion one saw, on television, an ambulance racing to the scene of an accident in the hope of finding a 'donor'. I think it was in connection with a proposed heart transplant that it was reported on radio (18.8.79) that the surgical team had been 'standing

---

[2] I have since learned that the subject of this experiment lived for 200 days. And, according to my notes, Radio 4, in the *Five P.M.* programme on 2nd December 1982, gave the further information that this kind of operation has been done for years in America, and also on 'brain dead' patients. In the *Horizon* programme, 3.10.83, we learned that if all heart patients were treated in this way the cost would represent about three-quarters of the present health budget.

around for hours'. (This is surely much more to be deplored than 'waiting around for dead men's shoes' – a practice in itself completely unethical!) The radio report went on to say that in a previous attempt 'the condition of the donor had improved'.

If transplants have to depend on a supply of 'brain dead' patients, has the stage been reached where there is a dependence on accidents to fulfil the need? Is it now a source of regret that seat belts have been introduced in cars, thus minimising the supply of 'brain dead' patients?

On 9th December 1983 – the day after I had written the above – the TV news item in *Sixty Minutes* was that because sufficient organs for transplants cannot be obtained in this country consideration is being given to buying them from the U.S. where they are surplus to requirements. It was explained that most doctors in this country avoid the emotional upsets involved in making decisions to 'donate'.

The ethics involved in transplant surgery need more careful consideration than appears to be given at present. If the practice is to continue, the first essential is, of course, that the donor's voluntary agreement, while in full possession of his/her faculties, must have been obtained. This may presuppose an eventuality such as a fatal accident (an eventuality which the donor may consider to be only a remote possibility). It is important that the donor gives his agreement in the full understanding that 'death' in certain modern medical practice, now includes 'brain' death, where the breath of life still exists, even though it is being sustained by artificial means. This artificial means, formerly described as 'life support', is now being described as 'ventilation of the body', which would seem to imply that the body has become a 'corpse' or 'dead body'.

There must be thousands of people around the world who now carry 'donor' cards indicating their willingness to 'donate' an organ or organs in the event of their meeting with a 'fatal' accident. Have they considered the implications of this for their nearest and dearest? The fact that accident cases are normally treated in hospital means that loved ones (relatives or friends) are unlikely to be near the 'brain dead' patients when an organ is being removed. This gives the whole operation a completely impersonal aspect, seemingly devoid of feeling and compassion. Its awfulness can only be understood by those who have sat by the bedside of a dying loved one, for whose remaining physical comfort no effort is spared until the breath of life departs.

As for those 'brain dead' patients, on life support machines, who have not given prior consent for an organ to be removed, it cannot be right to approach the next of kin for consent to remove an organ. On the one hand there is the trauma likely to be caused by such an approach, and on the other, where the patient may have been the victim of foul play, removal of vital organs could interfere with the requirements of any inquest deemed necessary. In fact, one case was reported where a coroner had to intervene before the operation for removal could begin.

More appalling is the suggestion now being put forward, as reported on the TV programme *Credo* (6th May 1984), that Parliament may be asked to introduce a Bill to allow organs to be removed from 'brain dead' patients who have not personally forbidden this to be done (by carrying a card to this effect? But who would know whether the card had been destroyed?)

The life support machine was surely first invented and applied in the interests of the patient where there was reasonable prospect that his/her life might be saved by this means. Should there come a point of no further hope for this patient, the step of withdrawing life support should be taken with the utmost reverence and not be postponed until after the removal of an organ in a situation of what can only be viewed as dispassionate clinical conditions.

In the year in which he died (of cancer) my husband entered in a small notebook some comments on radio and television talks. It appears that one talk given in January 1973 stressed the advantages, and ignored or minimised, the disadvantages, of modern technology. His terse comment reads: 'Technology, like fire, should be strictly controlled.'

Because a thing can be done, does this mean it must be done? In his autobiography the poet Edwin Muir wrote: 'In Helleran we did not know of that terrible and apparently real freedom which assumed that because everything was possible everything was allowable.'

It must be some fifty-five years since artificial insemination was introduced in the breeding of cattle. I well remember the impact made by the news, and how, in discussion, my friends and I speculated on future developments. The occasion of our discussion is as vivid in my memory as though it had taken place only yesterday. Forty years later, I found myself discussing the same subject with a friend living in the country who, with her husband and son, then worked a small croft. The conversation moved on to the subject of artificial insemination in humans, a practice which we both agreed to be immoral. I felt also that man was now deliberately interfering with the progress of evolution, with completely unknown consequences.

At this time I was reading *Memories and Meanings* by W. R. Matthews (former Dean of St. Paul's). The conversation described above had taken place in the afternoon of 25th August 1975, and in the evening I read to my great surprise:

> 'I know not why I was selected by the Archbishop to serve on his Commission, appointed in December 1945. "To consider the practice of human artificial insemination, with special reference to its theological, moral, social, psychological and legal implications, and to report to the Archbishop". . . . In 1961 I was involved in discussion of the same problems at a somewhat more advanced stage.
>
> '"Eugenics and the Family" was the subject of my Herbert Gray Lecture and the theories of some eugenists involved the technique of A.I.D. on a large scale. In this lecture I tried to convince my audience that we are in a situation with regard to the possible future of the human race which has no parallel in the past, because man is now able to take a decisive part in the evolution of the human race and "plan" the generations which will come after him; we are, in fact, confronted with the possibility that a new stage in the evolution of man is now beginning in which human intelligence and co-operation may help to produce a higher type of human being. . . .'

Who and where are the men and women qualified to act as God and decide which genetic traits should be preserved and which eliminated? And if opinions differ, as they must, who has the final say? *Quis custodiet ipsos custodes*? I am convinced that 'a higher type of human being' can only evolve when man is fully aware that he is part of a Plan for Creation and dependent on his Creator.

On 1st March 1980, the morning after I had written the last paragraph, it was announced on radio that five Nobel prize winners in America are said to have contributed to a 'sperm bank', and three women chosen for their high IQ will participate in an experiment to produce offspring of high intellect.[3] Immediately following this announcement, my morning reading began with these words from Psalm 72 (18, 19): 'Blessed be the Lord God . . . who alone does marvellous things!'

Peter Hebblethwaite, writing in *The Year of Three Popes*, has recorded that the Patriarch of Venice, before he became Pope John Paul I, com-

---

[3] Three years later, on 3rd August 1983, on the radio programme *Today*, it was disclosed that in America children are already being produced by this method.

mented on the technical progress which had made possible the birth of the first test-tube baby, but in considering the ethics involved in such medical intervention he drew attention to a conclusion reached by Pope Pius XII that where conception results from medical intervention in such a way that it becomes a *substitute* for sexual union it is not permissible.

Man has entered an area of experimentation which is likely to have disastrous and perhaps irreversible results. Take, for example, the case in 1981 of a woman said to be carrying the child of a friend, after being artificially inseminated with the sperm of the friend's husband. What does the future hold for such a child? And who would be deemed to be the real parents in a court of law?

Have we entered an age when single parenthood is to be regarded as the norm, the identity of a father becoming more and more difficult to establish where procreation is achieved by artificial insemination or the test-tube method?

Some years ago television programmes disclosed that 'cloning' – duplication of an individual – is not an impossibility for the future. Apparently this has already been done by veterinary science. The glimpse, on TV, of four lambs moving as though from a common impulse must have startled many viewers. (Barry Hines in *Did you see. . .?* acknowledged he was one such viewer.) Technical power of this kind in the wrong hands holds for me as many terrors as the nuclear bomb. Are we not now presented with the possibility that a race of automatons could ultimately be produced to influence the direction of human affairs? And would man now be prepared to *arrest*, by 'cloning', the process of evolution planned for him by his Creator?

Appalling also was the information (*Horizon*, B.B.C. 2, 15.11.82) that experiments were now regularly conducted in the mixing of cells from embryos of *different species*. What is the point, and what can possibly be gained from such experiments? I have always understood that in the animal world a horse mated with an ass produces a mule, which is usually sterile. And in the case of hybridisation of plants, is it not their tendency to revert to type? (Take the example of lupins.)

Radio and TV news programmes disclosed, on 3rd May 1983, that in Australia a human embryo, preserved for four months by freezing, had been successfully implanted in the uterus of the woman whose egg cells had helped provide a number of such embryos (subsequently frozen).

One of the doctors who spoke the same evening on *Nationwide* made what I felt was an inspired remark, that 'love was being overtaken by science'. He also expressed the fear that a Pandora's box had been opened. The self-same thought must have occurred to the minds of thinking people throughout the world.

To what use will frozen embryos be put when their legitimate prospective mothers do not require them? If it should be possible to preserve them for a hundred years, rather than the four months already achieved, would science aspire to conduct an experiment with them after that lapse of time? This could result in *arresting* (as would be the case with cloning) the natural evolution of man intended for him by his Creator.

On 8th November 1982, the topic discussed in *Horizon* (B.B.C. 2) was 'The Scientist and the Baby'. The following information was given in advance by the *Radio Times*: 'In obstetrics, as in every branch of medicine, medical research is opening up possibilities of treatment and care that the Health Service will not be able to afford.' When the programme was later broadcast, one of the speakers (a surgeon or consultant?) went even further in forecasting that advanced technology in medicine of the kind now being pioneered would, if allowed to develop, reach a stage when *no nation in the world would be able to afford it*! The cost of the Health Service in this country in 1983 was stated to be fourteen billion pounds a year. One wonders whether such expenditure, resulting, from among other things, advanced technology and expensive drugs, was ever envisaged by the founders of the Welfare State?

One can only assume that the skills developing so rapidly in the field of obstetrics have to a great extent been acquired by means of experiments on animals. In the *Horizon* programme referred to, an anaesthetised monkey was the subject of a step by step demonstration of the removal, and replacement, of a foetus (ostensibly the most nearly resembling a human foetus). Many people must, like myself, have viewed this with horror. We were not told whether the monkey made a satisfactory recovery after the operation (assuming that it did recover) while enduring unnecessary pain.

It is obvious that the *dilemmas* now being faced when trying to decide priorities in medicine and surgery have largely come about because of the rapid advance in technical skill acquired through experimentation on animals. Some of the problems, moral and legal, arising from modern technology in the area of childbirth – in particular, the *in vitro* technique – were raised, for the first time so far as I am aware, in the House of Commons on 30.3.82 (reported in *Yesterday in Parliament* 31.3.82). But are the implications of this kind of technology being further rigorously investigated? Do scientists consider fully, or give advice on, the possible dangers of putting into effect the results of their research? Some public awareness of the dangers does exist. Here is an extract from the columns of *The Shetland Times* of 18th February 1983: 'The (Health) Board discussed the Government's inquiry into human fertilization and embryology, but made no decision. Members were concerned that experiments in human reproduction should be controlled. Scientists conducting such experiments should make sure they keep within the bounds of the law and consider the ethics of the work they are doing.'

According to a news item on 9th November 1982, 'the controversial "test-tube baby" technology may shortly be taken over by private enterprise, so that the cost would no longer be a burden on the nation's taxpayers.' But though this might ease the burden on the nation's finances, would it not also remove from public view the developments taking place in this area of modern obstetrics? After all, was not the Abortion Act introduced on the grounds of abuse by private practice?

The question has to be asked again: because a thing can be done, must it be done?

This chapter ends, as it began, with a quotation from Albert Schweitzer's *Civilization and Ethics* (1923):

'In the history of ethical thought we wander in the innermost circles of world-history. Of all the forces which mould reality, morality is the first and foremost. It is the determining knowledge we must wring from thought. Everything else is more or less secondary.

'For this reason everyone who believes he can contribute something to help forward the ethical self-consciousness of society and of individuals has the right to speak now, although it is political and economic questions that the present day prescribes for study.'

Chapter 17

Artificial Intelligence?

It is only within recent months that I have realised that my closest friends through a long life have included a number with poetic gifts. The author of the following poem, Marjorie M. Ransom, was a dear friend who gave me constant love and support during the exacting years of the Second World War. She died, alas, in 1975.

The poem, written in September 1959, at a time when the subject of automation and the increasingly evident consequences of its development were occupying many minds, caught my eye recently when going through some papers, and I think it serves as an appropriate introduction to this chapter.

What is Automation?

After much investigation,
By a subtle infiltration
And a quick assimilation,
Born an age of Automation.

Fact collating delegation
With machine-made estimation,
By statistics correlation,
Offers hosts of information.

By its slick interpretation
Gives assuring confirmation,
Thus avoiding full frustration
And inspiring approbation.

Artificial Intelligence?

> Could it be hallucination,
> Optimistic aspiration,
> Falsely causing exultation,
> With resulting consternation?
>
> For the humdrum calculation
> Or repeating occupation,
> It's a splendid installation.
> Spare us, please, imagination!

It appears that in some branches of science there is growing speculation that a kind of 'super-intelligence' may eventually emerge, or evolve, out of the rapid and astonishing advances now being made in the computer industry.

A programme broadcast on Radio 3 on 14.3.83, in the series entitled *Machines with Minds*, drew attention to the fact that even twenty years ago there had been developed an 'intelligent' machine – 'Freddie the Robot' – which in its movements, e.g., in the course of an operation, moving a hand out of the way, could be said to have 'knowledge of itself', or a kind of intelligence. We were told that at the present day advanced engineering is producing another kind of robot, 'with purer artificial intelligence', modelling thought processes, with powers of reasoning, and indicating, possibly, the 'presence of sensory systems'.

But to what extent is the so-called intelligence of the robot really expected to develop? The robots at present operating so successfully in industry may be said to be motivated – by a kind of reasoning – to act in a certain way, but they can hardly be said to have consciousness[1] of their actions, except insofar as individual human consciousness may have influenced the information fed into them.

Artificial intelligence, so-called, may use a kind of reasoning, or handle concepts fed into it by people who are considered to be rational human beings, but this kind of reasoning can never be other than limited in scope because the information or concepts may be controversial, or even based on false premises which cannot be verified, and human experience is well aware of this. 'To know all knowledge leaves the truth unknown.'

For what purpose is it hoped to develop artificial intelligence? Are we being asked to visualise the day when life and death issues might be decided by an artificial 'super-intelligence'? In such an eventuality indi-

---

[1] consciousness – the totality of a person's thought and feelings (*Concise Oxford Dictionary*).

vidual responsibility would be completely abrogated. Is this really what is being aimed at? Another sorcerer's apprentice, but on a colossal scale, with powers such as were never dreamed of by any tyrant ancient or modern?

Of course, much depends on the meaning of the word 'intelligence'. Its implications are far wider than mere rationality, and seem to include 'flashes of inspiration' coming from who knows where, and influenced, possibly in some cases, by the feelings and emotions of the individual who receives them. A machine could never have such consciousness, the attribute of all normal human life, with human consciousness, along with the collective unconscious, governing all human thought and action.

It was Pascal's insight which caused him to declare: 'The heart has its reasons which reason does not know.' Surely this can be interpreted by saying that love has its reasons which reason does not know, and that there is something of God (Love) in each of us which should be reaching out all the while to the God of all Being.

A robot – according to the *Concise Oxford Dictionary* – is an 'intelligent and obedient but impersonal machine'. It is *inanimate* – an ingenious mechanism of man's creation, without the breath of life instilled by God in *His* creation. Man has not yet discovered the secret of life – nor will he.

It is being said that the artificial intelligence which the major powers of the world are competing to create, in order to have control of information, may develop to the extent that it operates on a level beyond the level of even the best human intelligence (Radio 14.3.83 and B.B.C.2 21.3.83), also that it might reach the stage where it would not condescend to talk to us, not being interested in the same things as us! For what purpose would it then exist? Would human intelligence simply rely on the conclusions and decisions of such a computer, addressing it with the words 'Thy Will be Done'! The implications must be obvious to anyone who believes in a God of Love who relies on his people to exercise *individual* responsibility for the future of His creation.

In the TV series *Village Earth* (29.3.83) we learned a little about Mexico's wide variety of cultures and languages. This telling comment was made at the end of the programme: 'It is sad that the only new language to emerge is one for computers and not for people.' Four days later, on 2nd April, I chanced upon this verse in John Heath Stubbs' poem 'To a Poet a Thousand Years Hence':

Artificial Intelligence?

Or do computers churn it out —
In lieu of Songs of War and Love,
Neat slogans by the State endorsed
And prayers to *Them* who sit above?

Chapter 18

The Mystery Beyond Investigation

'There is something mysterious in the universe which is in complicity with those who love nothing but the good.'
(Simone Weil – quoted by Philip Toynbee in *Part of a Journey*)

A chapter now devoted wholly to coincidences may seem preposterous, but it is suggested they should be viewed in the light of the above quotation. Is it not possible that those who in their life on earth 'loved nothing but the good' – Vagaland was such a one – may have been granted the privilege of communication with their loved ones, by means of thought processes?

In Vagaland's poetry there are frequent allusions to the supremacy of good, as interpreted by love, but most clearly and directly is the idea suggested in 'Night-Scented Stock', one of his last poems, where he speculates that:

> The thoughts of others who have truly loved us
> May flow towards us on the channelled air,

love here being used in its true sense as an attribute of God, emanating in its purest form from those who 'love nothing but the good'. Such loving sees only the good in the person loved, irrespective of all shortcomings, and is able to nourish that good.

What is termed as 'extra-sensory perception' remains a mystery beyond investigation in the field of science. The term E.S.P. is in itself inadequate, for, while individual perception or awareness is involved, the source of what is available to perception or awareness cannot be explored.

The personal experiences such as I have related are, by their very nature, unverifiable, their authenticity depending in the first place on the veracity of the person recounting them, and, even where this is not doubted, there remains the afore-mentioned impossibility of investigating the *source* of thought. Deep emotional stress undoubtedly heightens one's awareness of significant events, and I believe that, in my own case, an overwhelming sense of love and gratitude may have enabled communication from the unseen world to be maintained. The love which we have experienced in this world is not nullified at the time of death – it is a continuing, eternal force.

I understand that the present theory of science is that the emotions are located in the primitive brain, and in *The Ghost in the Machine* Arthur Koestler speaks of 'the need to integrate the rational and emotional modes of understanding', and he suggests that, 'poetry could be said to achieve a synthesis between the reasoning of the new cortex and the primitive, emotional ways of the old brain.' He speculates whether E.S.P. is 'an emergent level of supra-individual consciousness' *or* 'an earlier version of psycho-symbiotic awareness preceding self-awareness, which evolution has abandoned for the latter'.[1]

The second alternative has frightening implications. If psycho-symbiotic awareness is to be interpreted as awareness which includes all the emotions, and particularly the emotion of love, and if *self*-awareness is likely to suppress these emotions, mankind has certainly reached a dangerous stage in his evolution, with the added hazard that he is now attempting to direct it by scientific means!

From time to time the view is expressed that man's thinking may eventually be taken over by the computer. A computer without emotion, imagination, experiences . . . without consciousness?

In *Astride the Two Cultures*, edited by Arthur Harris, Professor Eysenck is quoted as having conceded that there may be people with extra-sensory perception, 'though this does not give any support to the idea of survival after death'. My conviction is that, although we can know nothing of the form of life after death, there is *mind* at work, with knowledge of our situation and influencing thought and action, thus providing evidence of survival. In *The World is a Wedding*, Canon Allchin has written: 'The world of time and the world of eternity are nearer to each other than we usually think. There is a good deal of coming and going between them.'

---

[1] Arthur Koestler's interest in the subject is demonstrated by the fact that in his will, in 1983, he bequeathed half a million pounds for investigation of the 'paranormal'.

Joan Forman in her book *The Mask of Time*, which is written from both the scientific and the religious point of view, seems to dismiss in a few words, as not significant, coincidences connected with reading. For me, these have been the most important and significant of all, and the only inference I can draw is that there are beings or minds, individually or collectively influential, surrounding us, with knowledge of what we are about to read, hear or see, and they are able to provide us with 'coincidental' thoughts beforehand.

In the same book it is suggested that coincidence may be due to 'a type of psychokinesis, by which a percipient encountering a particular incident which interests him, may then attract other references to ingredients of this incident. . . .' But is it conceivable that a thought in a person's mind could *attract* almost immediately afterwards the same thought in the printed word? In my experience the printed word in question may have been written many years ago by someone no longer inhabiting this planet!

I think it was Arthur Koestler who remarked that Providence has never been thought to have a sense of humour. I may say that my heart rejoiced in the humour indicated by the following 'coincidence' recorded on 3.9.75:

'While gardening I laid the rake in a safe position as I am always fearful that someone may step on it and get "knocked out". During a rest after lunch, I continued my perusal of one of my husband's books, a selection of Robert Frost's poems, and this is what I read:

The Objection to Being Stepped On

At the end of the row
I stepped on the toe
Of an unemployed hoe.
It rose in offence
And struck me a blow
In the seat of my sense.
It wasn't to blame
But I called it a name,
And I must say it dealt
Me a blow that I felt
Like malice prepense.
You may call me a fool
But *was* there a rule

The Mystery Beyond Investigation 115

> The weapon should be
> Turned into a tool?
> And what do we see?
> The first tool I step on
> Turned into a weapon.

Robert Frost lived to the ripe age of eighty-nine. I was glad to read recently that as long ago as 1913 he was encouraged in his poetry by Rupert Brooke and others. It was Rupert Brooke also who introduced Housman's poetry to his fellow students at Cambridge.

One morning some years ago, I recalled how in the early stages of my breakdown I had awakened one morning to hear the unmistakeable voice of my father (who had died several years previously) speaking the words 'Trust in God'. In his lifetime he had certainly never counselled me in these direct words. With him example was better than precept.

On this occasion recollection of the experience reminded me that one of his favourite Scottish songs was 'Ilka Blade o' Grass', by James Ballantyne, which begins:

> Confide ye aye in Providence, for Providence is kind,
>   An' bear ye a' life's changes wi' a calm an' tranquil mind.
> Tho' pressed and hemmed on every side, hae faith an' ye'll win through,
> For ilka blade o' grass keps its ain drap o' dew.

The following day, Sunday, I switched on television to listen to a discussion in the series *Christianity Explored*. Bishop Montefiore was at that moment explaining what faith in 'Providence' meant for him.

When editing my husband's poems in 1974 I endeavoured to supply as comprehensive a glossary as possible of the dialect words. With a few of these I had difficulty, which led me to search from time to time among our collection of Shetland books, some of which I hoped might have glossaries. One book which I prised from the bookshelves was *Rough Island Story* by a Shetland writer, William Moffatt, who had attended our local school at the beginning of the century, and whose book, in fact, is dedicated "To Happyhansel, a Seat of Learning". This, to my surprise and delight, though not provided with a glossary, gave me other information for which I had so far been looking in vain, namely, details of Faeroe fishing boats, or 'smacks' as they were called, about which my husband had written a short poem:

Faeroe fishin
Sooth-aest wind ida first o da Voar-time,
Smacks aa clair fir da Faeroe run;
Een be een, wi dir mainsails hystit,
Dey hadd awa fir da settin sun.
 Makkin on fir da Lille Dimun,
 Snuggit doon whin he blaas a gael,
Gengs Violet, Sylvia, William Martin,
 Magic, Mizpah, and Silver Belle.

Ower da Faeroe Bank dey gadder,
Smacks aa lyin at dir droags;
Eighty faddom ta rin da boddim,
Hyooks weel-baitit wi saatit yoags.
 Plenty o wark whin fish is takkin
 Wi a sleety shooer or a sunny spell,
Apo Violet, Sylvia, William Martin,
 Magic, Mizpah, and Silver Belle.

Plenty o wark, bit fun atweentimes
In ida freendly Faeroe toon;
Göd fishin, mair as twenty thoosand;
Dan, wi da hatches battened doon,
 (An maybe some kigs o Faeroe braandy
 Among da fish at dey hae ta sell),
Comes Violet, Sylvia, William Martin,
 Magic, Mizpah, and Silver Belle.

Of the Shetland fishing smacks named in this poem, four were from Skeld (the poet's birthplace) and two from Scalloway. The four from Skeld were called *Sylvia*, *Magic*, *Mizpah* and *Silver Belle*. The poet's Uncle Magnus, who died in 1965 at the age of eighty-seven, was a one-time crew member of the *Mizpah*; his father (as a young boy) and, later, his Uncle James, were crew members of the *Silver Belle*.

However, this chapter is being devoted to as many as possible of the strange occurrences, or sequences of events, which have left me in no doubt that they impinge on our consciousness *by design*.

---

clair – ready; snuggit doon – made fast; droags – sea anchors; faddom – fathom(s); yoag – horse-mussel.

The Mystery Beyond Investigation

In October 1975, on returning from Essex following the death of a lifelong friend, I stayed for a few days with her relatives in Aberdeen. On waking early one Sunday morning I struggled in vain to remember the name of the author of the play *The Bluebird*. My husband had referred to this book during his last illness, and I read it for the first time after his death. The author's surname I just could not recall, although I did come to the conclusion that his first name might be Maurice!

Here I may as well continue from my notes:

'In the evening four of us looked for half an hour at TV. At the end of the half-hour comedy which we had watched, Margaret was going to switch off the set when I noticed that the children's serial was about to follow and suggested it might be interesting. It turned out that the serial had reached a part called *Ballet Shoes*, in which children were rehearsing for a ballet based on the play *The Bluebird* by Maurice Maeterlinck, whose name I had struggled in vain to remember!

'It should be emphasised I had not seen a *Radio Times* for seven weeks, nor seen or heard about any children's programme in all this time. I believe this was yet another "occurrence" influenced in some strange way by my emotional state following the death of my friend in Essex.'

At home in Shetland, a little over a week later, I watched the TV programme *Mastermind*. One of the questions asked was 'From what is the colour sepia obtained?' the answer being 'the cuttlefish'. After the programme, almost the first sentence I read in *Point Counter Point* was: 'Sidney talked for the same reason as the hunted sepia squirts ink, to conceal his movements'!

Not a few coincidences have been connected with Bible readings! The small house to which my husband and I moved in 1970 had cedar panels under and above its windows, and one evening I chanced to meet one of the building contractors who had designed the house, consulted him as to how these panels should be treated, and was told: 'Paint them with red cedar dressing.' Prescribed reading next morning was from Jeremiah 22, v. 14 '. . . I will build a spacious house with airy roof-chambers, set windows in it, panel it with cedar and paint it with vermilion'!

In March 1976, when looking for a suitable hymn to play at the funeral service for a member of our church, I consulted a list of suggested hymns in *Congregational Praise* and was rather surprised to find included the hymn 'The Strife is O'er', which I had always thought applied only to

Easter Sunday and Christ's Resurrection. Two days later I heard an excerpt from the broadcast funeral service for General Montgomery. 'The Strife is O'er' was being sung!

More than once the 'tie-up' between events has concerned books and television. On 26th December 1976, I consulted my gardening books about the growing of clematis, when my attention was attracted to one of my husband's books – *A Herbal of All Sorts* by Geoffrey Grigson. Its opening pages referred the reader to a picture on page 33, 'Summer', by Guiseppe Arcimboldi (1527–1593). The picture I found to be truly arresting, for 'Summer' is shown as a man whose head and shoulders are composed wholly of fruit, plants, vegetables and flowers.

The same evening on television I watched a programme in which the Osmonds presented a song and dance act around an enormous bowl of soup. This developed into the bowl of soup taking on the proportions of a large pool. The Soup Fairy appeared, her head decorated by every conceivable kind of vegetable!

On 5th April 1976, in the *Ask the Family* television programme, the answer to one question was that the Duke of Cumberland was supposed to have written a death sentence on the back of a "nine of diamonds". Fifteen minutes after hearing this, I picked up *Poems of To-day* (Fifth Series) which I had brought from the library that morning, and read, in a poem by W. H. Auden, the lines:

> ... To rule was a pleasure when
> One wrote a death sentence
> On the back of the Ace of Spades and played on
> with a new deck.

To illustrate further the amusing nature of some of these occurrences, here is an account written down on 13th April 1976:

> 'My husband's sister-in-law, from Waas (my native village), called three days ago. In conversation she recalled some childhood memories and spoke of a shop owned at one time by a man known as "Willy Plenty". It appears that when asked if he had such and such an article in stock his reply was always "Plenty"!'
>
> 'This morning I collected a few subscriptions for the O. & Z. Association, and spent a short time with a lady who told me that her brother had recently sent a copy of *The Collected Poems of Vagaland* to a friend abroad. She identified the friend as being

grandson of the shopkeeper who used to be known as "Willie Plenty"!'

Of course, I am by no means alone in having the kind of experince which I describe! One probably common to us all is that we think of someone, for no apparent reason, and meet that person shortly afterwards. Or, perhaps, we meet someone whom at first glance we mistake for someone else, and then, a few paces further on, we meet that 'someone else'. One morning in January 1975, after three successive instances of mistaken identity, I met their 'originals' individually farther along the street. In my own case, these occurrences do seem to have been closely linked with my emotional state.

How does one account for this kind of experience on 2nd April 1975? I should mention that I very rarely consult medical books.

'I read in a medical book this morning that if a man drinks a pint of sea-water he must pass one pint and a half of water to get rid of the salt, and so runs a greater risk of dying from lack of water than a man who drinks nothing.

'On the 6.00p.m. news there were pictures of ships evacuating refugees from battle areas in Vietnam, and mention was made of a man seen to drink sea-water because of lack of fresh water, or of drinking fluid of any kind.'

I first began to record coincidences early in 1973 when both my husband and I had remarked on their 'strangeness'. During the whole of 1974 I was frequently aware that I seemed to be receiving guidance in the editing of his collected poems, and guidance I certainly needed, having undertaken in advanced years a task for which I had no previous experience. Because I worked late into the night, often long past midnight into the early hours, on this work, few of the accompanying coincidences were recorded, but one seems to have demanded to be written down:

'Shortly after my husband's death, in a letter to a friend, Sir John Betjeman indicated how helpful it would be to have a recording of Vagaland's dialect poetry. The idea that this might be produced concurrently with the collected poems appealed to me, and I consulted the Folk Society who were anxious to contribute a memorial to their former Secretary. At this stage a gramophone recording was contemplated, but a few days later the thought came to me that a cassette recording might be preferable.

'Next morning, a Sunday, when about to switch off the radio before going out to church, I chanced to hear a reference to a cassette recording of poetry by a firm in Kirkintilloch. I also heard Bryden Murdoch's name mentioned, and, not having time to linger and hear the rest of the programme, I decided to write to him. In response to my subsequent letter, I received from the Rev. Tom Veitch, Edinburgh, a complimentary cassette recording of his poetry, read by Bryden Murdoch. Both Mr. Veitch and Mr. Murdoch gave me very helpful advice on how to proceed.'

I think it could only have been a short while before this that cassette recording of Scottish poetry commenced to be made. At all events, the idea was new to me, and I was very grateful for the help to which I seemed to have been guided.

Sponsored by the Shetland Folk Society, the recording of some of my husband's dialect poems and songs was expertly undertaken by Mr. William Kay, and for the willing help given by him and the many friends who contributed their vocal talents my gratitude can never be adequately expressed.

Vagaland commemorated every wedding anniversary with a poem – in English, not dialect. 'Beach of Bright Pebbles' was written for New Year's Eve, 1959, and is quoted in full in another chapter. 'House of Memory' was the theme for our anniversary the following year. It seems to me that in these poems there is a purity of diction which is to be found in all his poetry, whether in English or in dialect.

> Now the sun rises late from cloudy blankets
>   And in the afternoon goes back to bed;
> To light the grey days there is little colour
>   Except the brands of sunset, burning red.
>
> Now are the hills and valleys, fields and meadows
>   Asleep beneath the spell of Winter's cold;
> But, in a little, Springtime will embroider
>   On Earth's green cloth the first bright threads of gold
>
> And every day will add another colour
>   And make for us a glowing tapestry,
> To add to others that we have already
>   Hanging within our House of Memory –

Our House of Memory, where we can linger
Among the scent of flowers, the soft haze
Of Summer, and the magic of spring-water,
And draw the curtains in the dull, cold days.

Another well-loved Shetland poet is Emily Milne, a former schoolmate. She had unique powers of observation, as evidenced by her knowledge of Shetland bird life, and wild life generally, all remembered in remarkable detail, although most of her adult life was spent in England far away from the islands. The title of her book of dialect poetry, *Wi Lowin Fin*, published in 1962, comes from her poem 'Da Mill', which has the line:

Da loch troot fled wi lowin fin

The Shetland name for the puffin is 'Taamie Noarie', and Emily Milne's poem 'Da Taamie Noaries' Bankit' (banquet) is a singular achievement, for here are given the local dialect names of almost every Shetland bird, and, in addition, the dialect names of countless fish, insects, weeds, etc., all of which are items on the menu for the birds' 'bankit'.

In May 1975, I had just finished reading this fascinating poem and turned to resume my reading of a library book called *House of Memory* by Richard Collier. The next chapter in the book was called 'Mr. Puffin'! Apart from my surprise at this coincidence, it occurred to me that Emily Milne's poem had truly been produced from *her* 'house of memory'. She had lived away from her native islands for some forty years.

Reflecting on the loss of so many of my contemporaries, I am reminded of an entry in my notebook on 30th September 1976:

'Having heard that the Prime Minister was to be interviewed by Robin Day in the TV programme *Tonight* at 10.45, I decided to "stay up" for this programme.

'Pressed twice, during the interview which followed, as to the certainty of the efficacy of present economic measures, the P.M. said twice that the only certain thing for us all was "death". Half an hour later, before I fell asleep, I read these words in "B and B", in an article by Christopher Hollis: ". . . Chaucer seems to have looked at the chances and changes of life with an amused, quizzical, unenthusiastic eye, certain only that, whatever happened, death must be the necessary, inevitable end of it all. . . ."'

However deep the suffering caused by the loss of a loved one – and the sense of desolation is indescribable – healing comes through the knowledge that love is timeless and eternal.

Modern man's understanding of time and space seems to progress steadily. On this subject, alas, I suspect the average child of elementary school age has knowledge far in advance of mine. But this does not lessen my interest, and I try to follow any discussions on radio or TV which may enlighten me. On 5th March 1977 it seemed to me that I was being taken a step or two forward in my understanding of the 'timelessness of time'. My notes read:

'Watched a TV programme, called *The Fantastic Journey*, "where a team of scientists disappears through a time warp into a different dimension where past meets future". A young boy in the story, son of one of the scientists, is a twin, with a brother elder by a few minutes. He is told that if he was living in London, and was phoning his twin brother in Tokyo, that brother would then be a day older than himself!

'Began reading tonight a book about William Blake, and read these lines from Blake's poem 'Auguries of Innocence':

> To see a World in a Grain of Sand
> and a Heaven in a Wild flower
> Hold Infinity in the Palm of your hand
> and Eternity in an hour.

'Then, later this evening, in *The Listener*, the following words occur in one of a series of Lent talks given by Stephen Verney, Canon of Windsor: "Generally, we are so busy keeping our engagements according to clock time that we exclude this awareness of timelessness, but when somebody you love has died, the barrier between those two worlds grows very thin, and a new pattern of events is set free to happen around us. As a friend, Raymond Panikkar, said to me, "The time of death is the death of time."'

Occurrences on 12th January 1976, were in a lighter vein:

'At breakfast I wondered about the origin of the words of "The Grand Old Duke of York". An hour later, on the bus which provides transport for the disabled, one of the children sang a few bars of a tune which I could not immediately identify, but which the driver told me was "The Grand Old Duke of York"! Reading in "B and B" in the evening, I find Auberon Waugh commencing his review of a book by saying that the author's preface might be described as the "Grand Old Duke of York" approach to writing a book!'

It will be noticed that most of the coincidences described have been connected with my reading, as was this one:

'30.3.75. Began to read last night a book by Martin Gilkes, *A Key to Modern English Poetry*, which I found when tidying our bookshelves. In the book were discussed the poets of the 1914–1918 War, with particular attention to Siegfried Sassoon's poetry written towards the end of that war. In the *World at One* programme today, some poems which have emerged from the troubles in Northern Ireland were read, the speaker wondering whether the situation there might produce "another Siegfried Sassoon".'

As I write, on 29th April 1980, there is an up-to-date amusing coincidence to relate. Yesterday evening I read for the first time George Orwell's essay on 'Politics and the English Language', which is included in the Penguin edition of *Inside the Whale and Other Essays*, a book which my husband may have bought in the 1970s. I was intrigued by the following sentence and dwelt on it for some time: 'Another example' (of metaphors twisted out of their original meaning) 'is *the hammer and the anvil*, now always used with the implication that the anvil gets the worst of it. In real life it is always the anvil that breaks the hammer.'

This morning I listened to the *Tuesday Call* radio programme, dealing with countryside and coastal bird life, and heard an account, contributed by a listener, of a novel method used by a thrush for getting a snail out of its shell. The ornithologist dealing with listeners' questions explained that the bird normally breaks the snail's shell by banging it against an *anvil*, such as a rock, stone, etc. I heard the word 'anvil' with difficulty and realised that my reading the day before had helped me to identify it!

And now, on 30th April, as I return to my typewriter to resume where I left off yesterday, I am feeling more than ever impressed by the significance of the source of thought. Yesterday evening I watched the television programme *The Black and the Gold*, with Iain Cuthbertson as narrator. The progress made by technology in order to satisfy the worldwide demand for oil is particularly impressive when one is familiar with the dangers of the seas which surround Shetland. The TV presentation of this advanced technology, fraught with constant danger and requiring such concentration that men can be engaged on it for only limited periods of time, left me thinking that these conditions may allow little or no time for thought of what may lie beyond the present world when our time comes to leave it, and it seemed likely that the personal convictions about which I have been trying to write might have no meaning for some people, and possibly even be open to ridicule. This morning, however, Richard Sims, speaking in *Thought for the Day*, has drawn attention to the ever-growing evidence of a search and longing for a source to supply spiritual needs in a world in which technology predominates.

I am sure there must be many an unspoken prayer in the minds of the brave men working out there on the oil rigs.

Chapter 19

Island Magic

Probably one of the most photographed views in Shetland is that which can be seen from the road which climbs the side of Weisdale Hill. So enthralling is this view, looking southwards to the very tip of Shetland, Fitful Head, that a stopping-place for cars was provided years ago. With ever varying weather and light conditions the scene presents a fresh appeal on each visit, and on our journeys westwards my husband and I seldom missed an opportunity to stop and admire, and to try to capture once more on film some of the magic.

The West Isles (Da Wast Isles, in Shetlandic) are central to the vista, and for us held a somewhat special attraction as friends in Scalloway had on two separate occasions taken us by motorboat to visit them, and on both occasions we had been able to land on Hildasey, long uninhabited like the rest of the smallest of this group of islands. The two largest, Burra Isle and Trondra, still maintain a thriving population, and are now connected by bridges to the mainland of Shetland.

My husband's grandmother had been born in Hildasey, and, after a little exploration on our first visit, we believed we identified the ruins of what had once been her home. On the island there is a granite quarry, the stone from which, we learned, had been ferried all the way to Australia. I am not sure whether work stopped because of deterioration in the quality of the granite, or was it, as seems more likely, that the venture proved quite uneconomic?

Impressions of our visit are preserved in the poem 'The West Isles[1] written for our anniversary at the end of that year (1957):

---

[1] Unfortunately, when editing the *Collected Poems* I omitted the third and fourth verses of this poem which had been written on the back of the Anniversary card!

Sunlight sparkles on the wave-tops;
Small white clouds bedeck the blue;
As the boat moves out from the pier at Blacksness
Isle after isle comes into view.
Isles of the West! They lie before us –
Gem-stones set in a sun-gilt sea –
Oxna, Papa, Burra, Havra,
   Linga, Langa, and Hildasey.

Hildasey, with granite boulders,
Grey of rock and green of turf.
The folk who toiled and manned the haaf-boats
Brave no longer the circling surf –
Surf that even in calmest weather
Tells of the power of the mighty sea,
Girdling ever, in peace or anger,
   Linga, Langa, and Hildasey.

Homes are empty, crofts grass-covered;
Still the beaches edge the shore,
Beaches of stones that men have gathered
And built to form a level floor
– A challenge still, a brave reminder,
Once o'erspread with spoils of the sea,
When men would sail to the far-haaf fishing
   From the little haven of Hildasey.

White foam breaks around the Cheynies;
Sunset colours tinge the skies –
Pink of roses and fire of opals
Over the place where Foula lies.
The boat's head turns as light is fading;
Dusk is coming across the sea.
We watch them changing into dreamland
   – Linga, Langa, and Hildasey.

In the third verse the reference is to the beaches where fish were dried. The Cheynies are other small islands in the group.

To the east of the south Mainland of Shetland lies the island of Mousa, with its Pictish Broch challenging the imagination as to the manner of life of Shetland's ancient inhabitants. From such a starting point Vagaland commenced his well-loved poem, 'The Broch of Mousa', which traces the history of Shetland down the centuries to the 1950s when the islands were suffering a period of depression and depopulation. But the Broch has witnessed the islands' many changes of fortune, and in the closing verse a note of near despair changes to a note of optimism and encouragement. In my opinion this epic poem deserves a place alongside others highly regarded in English literature.

> Green is this isle beneath the summer sun
>   That tips the waves with gold;
> But, with a cloak of lichen covered o'er,
> The Broch of Mousa stands upon the shore,
>   Lonely, and grey, and old.
>
> Ages ago it challenged all who came,
>   Its walls and outworks manned.
> The Painted People ruled o'er many a Broch,
> By storm-swept pinnacle or sheltered loch,
>   In an embattled land.
>
> The men whom Roman arms could not subdue,
>   Who built this Northern hold,
> Whose glass-smooth boats like sea-birds skimmed the foam
> And flouted all the majesty of Rome,
>   Their tale has long been told.
>
> For some pressed southward, when the Roman tide
>   That washed these shores was spent;
> The few who lingered helped to form the weft
> Of a new Island-people, and have left
>   This Broch, their monument.
>
> So passed the Picts, their ways, their thoughts, their songs;
>   To earth they have returned;
> History has unrolled another page,
> Another group of actors filled the stage,
>   Where once the beacons burned.

This Broch has seen them surging through the Sound,
    The long-ships, one by one,
Bringing Torf Einar west across the seas,
Or sailing over to the Hebrides
    With Olaf Tryggvason.

The seas to Vinland and to Miklagarth[2]
    By Viking keels were scored;
They passed by Mousa, fresh from Norway's slips,
The brightly-coloured, dragon-headed ships,
    Clean-built, and many oared.

Gone are the Vikings from the Northern sea,
    The Skald with golden mouth,
The old Norn tongue, and many an ancient right,
Submerged beneath the wave of feudal might
    Advancing from the South.

Far from the land that once was theirs have sailed
    Men of the Island race.
Where flies the Snow Goose, or the migrant Tern,
Where grows the Wattle, or the Southern Fern,
    Is their abiding place.

Few are the fishing boats, untilled the ground,
    The earth o'ergrown with weeds;
Already in the Islands darkness falls
On homes deserted, and on ruined walls;
    The tide of life recedes.

This Broch has stood for twice a thousand years
    And watched men come and go.
The tide is ebbing out through Mousa Strait;
No doubt but it will turn and those who wait
    Will see the waters flow.

---

[2] Vinland – in the New World, but scholars have not yet agreed where; Miklagarth – the Norse name for Constantinople.

Island Magic

From the attic skylight of my childhood home there was a clear view of the island of Vaila lying across the mouth of the voe of Waas and so creating a natural harbour to which in those times many a fishing craft frequently ran for shelter.

There is a poem about this island written in the nineteenth century by J. Sands and included in his book *'King James' Wedding and Other Rhymes'* published in 1888, which gives an illuminating and, at times, amusing insight into life on the island as he saw it at that time.

Vaila

'The rain it raineth every day'
Varied by gales with hail and spray,
Small pleasure now it is to stray
   Upon the cliffs of Vaila.

Yet let me paint in homely style
A picture of this little isle, –
In length and breadth about a mile,
   Yet large enough, is Vaila.

The South and West confront the deep,
And there the crags are high and steep,
Yet broken billows often leap
   Above the rocks of Vaila.

And when the wintry tempests blow
The sea breaks on the stacks like snow,
And yeasty froth fills every *gio*
   Around the coast of Vaila.

Then spin-drift mingles with the air,
And all the ground is wet and bare
And quadrupeds but poorly fare
   For many months in Vaila.

The shaggy ponies, lean and weak,
The pebbly beach for sea-weed seek,
And crunching tangles in their cheek
   Support their lives in Vaila.

Within a manor house I dwell,
Erected, as escutcheons tell,
Long since by one Sir John Mitchell,
   And called 'the Haa' in Vaila.

The population is but small,
And numbers twenty-two in all;
One man and many maids are tall,
   And all are strong in Vaila.

Although the men can use the spade,
And help with it to earn their bread,
Yet fishing is the favourite trade,
   When weather suits in Vaila.

But weather does not always suit,
And then they patch or sole a boot,
Or make a *rivlin* for their foot,
   Or mend their lines in Vaila.

But when the fish are to be caught,
Then bolder men are not afloat
Than those who launch a six-oared boat
   And dash to sea from Vaila.

Though winds be strong and waves be high,
Across the rolling tide they fly,
Whilst calm, but watchful is the eye
   Of every man from Vaila.

They luff her up, or keep away,
And with the raging surges play,
Whilst o'er the gunwale pours the spray,
   But scares no man from Vaila.

And when they run before the gale
They watch the gusts and dip the sail,
And with a wooden shovel bail
   The boats that go from Vaila.

---

rivlin – sandal made of raw hide.

Island Magic

In Spring, when fish approach to spawn
And lines must from the deep be drawn,
The crews arise before the dawn
    And hurry off from Vaila.

Through rain or sleet they leave the shore,
And toss at sea ten hours or more;
Their rest is short, their labour sore,
    But none complains in Vaila.

Death on a billow-top may stand,
With dart in his uplifted hand,
But cannot daunt the hardy band
    That work the boats of Vaila.

None here a doctor need employ,
For all the best of health enjoy;
And Christie Thomson[3] like a boy
    Enjoys his food in Vaila.

Although eight years beyond fourscore
He still has strength to pull an oar,
And labours hard upon the shore
    With spade and flail in Vaila.

In Foula he was born and bred,
And though no books he ever read
He has more knowledge in his head
    Than any man in Vaila.

The knots in wood engage his mind,
And which will raise up gales of wind
If built in vessels he can find
    And show the men of Vaila.

He also has the gift or knack
When *luck* has left a boat or smack,
By magic arts to bring it back,
    Though few believe in Vaila.

---

[3] Christie Thomson, born in 1796, was eighty-eight years of age when the poem was written in 1884.

No Sabbath bell the island reaches,
No preacher ever comes and preaches;
Some shift their shirts and some their breeches
    To mark the day in Vaila.

I've lived in places in my time
Where grew the orange and the lime,
But I prefer the bracing clime
    And breezy cliffs of Vaila.

Here let me live, and when I die
Below the sea-pinks let me lie,
Where billows break and sea-fowl cry
    Upon the crags of Vaila.

Other versions of Sands's poem exist, containing lines not included in the above. It seems a pity that one verse in particular was omitted:

What splendid views by sea and land
The wild indented crags command,
The Isle of Foula, peaked and grand,
    Delights the eye from Vaila.

Foula lies some twelve miles to the west of Vaila and the mainland of Shetland. In his dialect poem 'Da Tree Isles' (the three islands) Vagaland dwells with nostalgia on the depopulation of Vaila, Linga (a tiny island between Vaila and the mainland of Shetland) and Foula, but concludes with a note of hopefulness which seemed reasonable enough before the advent of the nuclear age?

Da Isle o Linga is quiet an paecefil
Dim-green anunder da asky sky,
An sheddit here an dere wi purple
Whin da Simmer days is wearin by.
An weel I mind foo we wid aandoo
Trowe da Soond o Linga mony a nicht
An mak fir haem whin da lift wid mirken
An da folk ida isle pat up dir licht.

---

asky – misty; sheddit – shaded; foo – how; aandoo – row slowly;

Island Magic

Der a stur ida Voar wi tirriks comin
Ta bigg dir nests alang da ayre,
Bit da folk at wis wint ta bide in Linga
Dey göd awa, an cam back nae mair.

Awa ta da Sooth is da banks o Vaila;
Hit's dem at shalters da Voe o Waas,
Wi da ocean brakkin white apo dem
Whin a ragin gael fae da Sudderd blaas.
Dey wir mair as a score o folk in Vaila
Ta wirk da crofts an drive da haaf,
An dey wir as happy ita dir Island
As some at tocht dey wir better aff.
An noo da Isle is bricht wi banks-flooers
An da Simmer sea is bricht as weel,
Bit hit's lang an lang fae da beach o Vaila
Wis scordit be da Haaf-men's keel.

Whin da day is ower, and da sun is sunken
Below da Wastern ocean's rim,
Dan Foula lies apo da skyline,
A violet clood ida Simmer Dim.

We dönna kyin whan da first men laandit,
What boat first gained da shore at Ham,
Bit we kyin at der bön folk in Foula
Fir a thoosand years, fae da Veekings cam.
An we winder, as da nicht is comin,
An da rose-licht dims ower Foula's peaks,
'Will dis be da sam as idder places
Whaar no a single shimley reeks!'

Woven wi treeds o licht an shadow
We see da pictir o da past,
An noo hit seems at life is ebbin,
Ebbin awa fae da Isles o da Wast.

Voar – spring; tirriks – terns; ayre – beach; stur – stir; Sudderd – South; Dey wir – There was; drive da haaf – sail to deep sea fishing; banks-flooers – sea pinks; der bön – there have been; shimley – chimney.

It seems – bit wha can see da future?
Folk micht faa tired o da wirld o strife
An come ta bide whaar eence afore dem
Men lived a less oonsettled life.
Forsaken Isles! Da Aidge o da Wirld!
In days ta come dey weel micht gie
Ta men an baests an birds tagyidder
Life, an a place o sanctuary.

I had just typed the foregoing when I received a card announcing the birth of a daughter, Vaila, to young friends living in the south of England. The origin of this first-name, or fore-name, is familiar enough to those who have associations with our islands, but it may not be known to the many others who have adopted the name simply because they find it attractive. My eldest sister, Vaila, is believed to be the very first to be so named. She was born on 3rd May 1904.

Did the last four lines of the poem about the three isles, one wonders, sow the seeds of an idea which was mooted in *The Shetland Times* of 11th November 1983?

'Earlier this year, three women from the peace camp came to Shetland to give a series of talks about their life at the camp and while they were here paid a visit to Vaila and expressed an interest in buying the island.'

It would be a lucky island, of course, which escaped the terrors of a nuclear holocaust, or even the horrors of a so-called conventional war. The essence of meaning in the poem is, I think, that values for living need to be radically changed in this world of strife.

In his poem 'Meadowsweet' Vagaland assumes the role of an early Viking seafarer, who while 'tugging upon the oar' (of a longship?) reveals his innermost thoughts and feelings to a fellow oarsman. Even this early Viking seems to have had a favourite island – in this case probably Unst, Shetland's most northerly isle, for it was here on a warm summer evening that we saw an exuberant growth of meadowsweet, which inspired the poem.

Geoffrey Grigson in *The Englishman's Flora* tells how the word 'Meadsweet goes back at least to the fifteenth century (cf. the German *Madersuss. . .*; and it is clear that originally it was not the plant of the

---

tagyidder – together.

meadow or the sweetness of the meadow, but the plant used to flavour mead.'

Meadowsweet

Long have I bent and tugged upon the oar:
Long have we sailed into the sunset light,
Or steered by starflame in the heart of night.
Einar, when you go for'ard will you pour
Me out a horn of mead, for I am cold
And it will warm me; it is honey-gold,
The wild-bees' wealth of Summer flowers untold,
Flavoured with Meadowsweet.
Full well do I remember Erik's Hall,
The blue smoke-dragons coiling by the wall,
The wood-fire's glowing heat;
And how we sat and talked as mead went round
Of Bjarni Herjulfsson, the land he found
Far to the Westward, where none else has been;
Pleasant it is to see what few have seen;
No Northman's foot has trod that Western strand,
But Leif, I trow, will land.
Often he spoke of it in Winter nights,
When we were guests of Olaf, Norway's King.
And saga-men would speak, and skalds would sing
Of voyages and fights.
The drinking-horn would pass from hand to hand;
Strong is the Yule-mead brewed in Olaf's land,
And flowers of Meadowsweet are steeped in it.
Of all the stories told at these Yule-feasts,
Of far-off lands, strange men, or wondrous beasts,
To fire men's blood, or set them dreaming, yet
I do remember best the Priest who spoke
And told us of the White Christ, He who broke
The Power of Odin, and of Thor and Frey.
The White Christ, who from Heaven came down to Earth
In the dark days of Yule, His wondrous birth
Proclaimed by Angels that first Christmas Day,
The same who watched the sea break o'er His ship
And bade the waves be still,

Night-Scented Stock in Bloom?

Not like a Warlock, weaving spells profound,
But like a man, facing a savage hound
That, crouching, does his will,
I am Christ's man now, and I fain would know
More of Him and that land where men will go
When life is over, fears and hopes and dreams;
Not to Valhalla's clashing swords and shouts,
The endless fighting and the drinking bouts,
But to green pastures and to peaceful streams
Where men may rest, having no need of gold,
Weary of night and darkness, pain and cold.
The wind blows chill. Glad am I of this mead
To warm my blood. Whate'er our land-fall be,
I think it will not seem more fair to me
Than was the island that I chanced to see
In Summer-time, for it was fair indeed,
The grasses woven with flowers, streams murmuring,
And by the water grew the Meadowsweet.
In all my thirty years of wandering
I have not seen a place I liked so well,
And, when this voyage is over, I shall go
Back to that dell in Hjaltland which I know.
Hard though it be the future to foretell,
If luck goes with me, I again may greet
The maid I chanced one Summer-day to meet
Among the Meadowsweet.

Chapter 20

The Seasons

The first house in which we lived after our marriage in 1953 had the advantage of facing a public park, and there we took many a walk all the year round, accompanied by our little Shetland sheepdog, Susie. Early in March each year we would explore the rocky bank at the far end of the park, looking for signs of Spring, which for us was deemed to be heralded by the appearance of the first golden yellow flowers of the coltsfoot (L. *Tussilago farfara*). These flowers get their name from the shape of the leaves which subsequently develop and often grow to an enormous size in the late summer and autumn.

I am happy to say that Vagaland's dialect poem 'Tuslag', which follows, appears in *The Oxford Book of Scottish Verse*, edited by John MacQueen and Tom Scott, and published by the Oxford University Press in 1966.

>Wi da lentenin days ida first o da Voar
>Da Mairch wind comes agyin ta da door
>At da black frost stekkit wi bolts an bars,
>An reesles him open apo da harrs.
>
>We wait, whin da door is open wide,
>Fir life ta come ta da world ootside.
>Ee day, wi a glöd atween da shooers,
>We see da first o da Tuslag flooers.

Voar – Spring; stekkit – shut (cf. Icelandic '*Stekit*'); reesles – wrests; harrs – hinges; glöd – sunshine.

Whaar last year's girse lies bleached an dowed
Dey sheen laek a nevfoo o yallow gowd.
Whin we see dem apo da eart we kyin
At da Voar is here wi his arles agyin.

Dey're a sign ta men at da Voar can gie
Plenty ta dem at'll earn dir fee
Be da toil o dir haands an da sweat o dir broo,
Wi kishie, an spade, an harrow, an ploo.

Whin dey're kyerried an borrowed and spread an shölled
An delled da leys an harrowed da möld,
Dey can say at last, 'We're döne wir best;
Lord send göd wadder ta dö da rest.'

Dey'll be mael an taaties, an maet fir kye,
Ta pey fir wir wark, an we'll get firbye,
As da year gengs on wi da sun an shooers,
Da colour an scent o a million flooers.

Vagaland's bilingual gift is demonstrated when his dialect poem 'Tuslag' is set alongside his English poem 'April' – a translation from the French of Remi Belleau.[1] Without having seen the original mediaeval poem one senses that its mood, metre and simplicity have been preserved:

> Kind April, laughter of love
>   from above,
> Where Venus dwells in the sky;
> From the earth perfume distils
>   and it fills
> The halls of the gods on high.

---

[1] Remi Belleau (1528–1577): one of the Pleiade group of poets formed in France in the reign of Henry III. The group included Ronsard.

---

nevfoo – handful; arles – token payment; kishie – peat-basket; borrowed – barrowed (wheeled); shölled – shovelled; delled – delved; wadder – weather; mael – meal; taaties – potatoes; maet – meat; kye – cattle; firbye – as well.

Most gracious month, it is you
    who anew
Those exiled migrants bring –
The swallows that here and there
    in the air
Are the harbingers of Spring.

Fair season, when violets grow,
    and aglow
Are the briar and pink-flushed may.
Lilies and roses untold
    now unfold
Their Springtime dresses gay.

In November 1982, the original poem by Remi Belleau was kindly traced for me by the Aberdeen University booksellers – James G. Bisset Ltd. It appears to have been included in a work, *La Bergerie*, which Belleau published in 1572 – an account of two days spent in the country at the Chateau de Joinville, home of the Duchess of Guise[2] – in which descriptions of countryside and architecture are interspersed with a number of lyrics, one of which, 'Avril', has thirteen verses, from which it transpires that only three were selected by Vagaland for translation:

Avril, la grâce et le ris
    De Cypris,[3]
Le flair et la douce haleine;
Avril, le parfum des dieux,
    Qui des cieux
Sentent l'odeur de la plaine;

C'est toi, courtois et gentil,
    Qui d'exil
Retires ces passagères,
Ces arondelles qui vont
    Et qui sont
Du printemps les messagères.

---

[2] Mother of Mary, Queen of Scots.

[3] Cypris – one of the surnames of Venus.

> *L'aubépine et l'aiglantin*
> *Et le thym,*
> *L'oeillet, le lis et les roses*
> *En cette belle saison*
> *A foison*
> *Montrent leurs robes écloses.*

The poem seems not only to have lost nothing in translation, but may even have gained?

Now in my eighties, memories of early childhood spent in the quiet village of Waas keep coming back to me. In the winter time, when darkness fell early – in the heart of winter, darkness comes down before three in the afternoon – we small children would find our way by winding road without even the help of a 'blinkie' (torch). When the moon shone bright, our path was, of course, well lit for us, and, if the night was still, the star-decked heavens were over and around us, so familiar that I sometimes took them for granted.

Not so Vagaland, who grew up in the same village in those distant days, and whose observation of the stars and their movements must have been as keen as his delight in the landscape around him. Here is his dialect poem "Starn-Licht":

> Hit's lichtsome in a Winter nicht
> Ta watch da Seeven Starns shift
> An mark da ooers aboot da bricht
> Yöle-blinker ida Nordern lift.
>
> Whin seed is set an coarn is saan,
> You look apo da sheenin Ploo;
> Trowe aa da fine Voar nicht he's gyaain
> Aroond da Starn at staands sae true.
>
> As Simmer ends, you stack your paets;
> You tak da dug an caa your sheep;
> Da Dipper ida starry gaets
> Is heeldin, whin you faa asleep.

---

lichtsome pleasant; ooers – hours; Yöle-blinker – Pole star; coarn – oats; Ploo – Plough; Voar – Spring; starn – star; paets – peats; caa – drive; Dipper – Ursa Major (the Great Bear); heeldin – tilting.

> You hae ta toil, an hird, an ripe,
> Till aa da wark o Hairst is döne;
> An dan you sit an smok your pipe
> An Sharlie's Kyert still turns abön.
>
> You see da haemly starns up by
> Muvvin aroond ita dir place –
> Writin a promise ida sky
> At Voar and Hairst sall never saece.

No wonder that Vagaland commented, in one of his poems, in much later life when living in Lerwick:

> Bit electreecity is laek
> ta slokk da starns abön.

In recognition of help given for an article in *The Reader's Digest*, Vagaland was presented with a copy of their *World Atlas*. Browsing through its pages a few years ago, I found one devoted to 'The Stars Around Us', and amused myself for quite a while studying the North Star and other stars in relation to it. In my 'quiet hour' next morning the first words in the reading specified for that day were: 'Let it once be fixed that a man's one ambition is to fit into God's plan for him, and he has a North Star ever in sight to guide him steadily over any sea, however shoreless it seems.'

Besides the light from moon and stars to be enjoyed in those far-off days of country life, there were frequently the 'Northern Lights' or 'Aurora Borealis', to give them their official name, providing an awe-inspiring spectacle. 'Prettie Dancers' they were also sometimes called locally. 'Nordern Lichts' is a poem which expresses the sense of awe which can be evoked by this phenomenon in the Northern Sky:

> Da voe is lyin silver
> An da tide is at da browst;
> Da calm o midnicht gadders
> Ower da boats ita da nowst,

---

hird – gather in 'corn'; ripe – reap (potatoes); 'Sharlie's Kyert' – Charles's Wain!; slokk – extinguish; browst – turn; nowst – where boat is kept.

Da peerie felt-röfed hooses
  An da tekkit byres an barns,
Wi strae a golden glimmer
  Doon below da glansin starns.

Da lift begins ta mirrl
  Wi da Prettie Dancers bricht;
Dey're muvvin up an shiftin
  In a aze o trowie licht.
Whaar brodd across da Heevins
  Lies da baand as white as mylk,
You tink you hear da skruffel
  O dir lang, green goons o sylk.

Dey tell da waanderin sailor
  At he böst ta mak a vaige;
Dey bid him rise an follow
  Dem oot ower da far haaf's aidge.
Da saisons dey maan alter
  An da ootland-fool maan flee
Da gengin fit maan traivel
  Fir der somethin aye ta see.

Dir örie licht is playin
  Ower da shoormil at da ayre
Whaar sits a selkie-maiden
  Wi da green lowe in her hair.
Dir örie licht maks shadows
  Oot an in aboot da broos,
An Peerie Folk is hoidin
  Ida yaird among da skroos.

Dey spaek wi different voices
  Ta da folk at looks at dem;
Da tane may see da wirld
  An da tidder bide at haem;

---

strae – straw; lift – sky; mirrl – vibrate; aze – glow; trowie – supernatural; böst ta – must; vaige – voyage; maan – must; ootland-fool – migrant bird; fit – foot; shoormil – part of shore washed by waves; ayre – small beach; selkie – seal; Peerie Folk – these would be mice and other small creatures; skroo – a stack of corn (oats).

> Bit even if you traivel
> Fir a hunder thoosand miles,
> You mind da Prettie Dancers –
> Dey're da magic o da Isles.

Vagaland's poem was first published in 1952. It is interesting to compare his lines:

> You tink you hear da skruffel
> O dir lang, green goons o sylk

so descriptive of the 'sound' of the 'Northern Lights', with the following also quoted by W. Petrie in his book *Keoeeit: Story of the Aurora Borealis*:

> The cauld blue North was streaming forth
> Her lights, wi' hissing eerie din
> (from 'A Vision', by Robert Burns)

> They writhed like a brood of angry snakes
> Hissing and sulphur pale

> They rolled around with a soundless sound
> Like softly bruised silk
> (from 'The Ballad of the Northern Lights'
> by Robert Service)

One wonders how many of the world's inhabitants of today have, or take time, to observe the Aurora Borealis in the Northern, or the Aurora Australis, in the Southern, hemisphere. Most city dwellers hurrying along brilliantly lit streets may be completely oblivious of the star-studded heavens above them. I know this, having been a city dweller for much of my own life. And, even in the country, where so much travelling is done by car, the opportunity to 'stand and stare' may be missed. I like to think that the poem 'Nordern Lichts' may recover some of the lost magic for those who have memories like mine.

Chapter 21

'The Star . . . Whose Worth's Unknown'
(Shakespeare, Sonnet CXVI)

Nearly every number of *The New Shetlander*, which made its first appearance in March 1947, contained a poem by Vagaland. For his last contribution, to the December 1973 issue, he asked me to make a choice between two poems, both in English. In less heartrending circumstances, for we shared the knowledge that his illness was terminal, I would have chosen *'Beau Chevalier'*, a translation from the French of Alfred de Musset:

>What will you do, young knight-at-arms,
>   'mid war's alarms, when forth you fare?
>Know you not that the night is dreary,
>   and the earth weary, and full of care?
>
>You who believe a love forsaken
>   is quickly shaken from heart and thought;
>Alas! you searcher after glory,
>   your own brief story endureth not.
>
>When you fare forth, young knight-at-arms,
>   'mid war's alarms, what will you do?
>I go to weep, for my heart is broken,
>   like the love-token I shared with you.

A friend in Switzerland sent to my husband in 1969 the poems of Vio Martin, one of which was entitled *'C'est Parce Que Nous Nous Aimons'*, which remained the title of Vagaland's dialect version:

Hit's love at maks da lyin snaa
Apo da stubble look sae pure:
Nae idder thing bit love, A'm sure.

Hit lies sae deep ower every place
Whaar folk eence toiled till life wis by,
Ower rigg an oot-run, bank and blett,
An ower da kirkyard whaar dey lie.

Hit's love, an no anidder thing,
At maks da snaa look winderfil,
An we'll geng oot an truck a gaet
Whaar aa da eart is lyin still.

An eftir wis, hit weel may be
Da moarn'll see anidder twa
Followin wir fit-marks trowe da snaa.

Can it be that these two love poems have a poignant appeal for me alone? Besides the two foregoing translations from the French, poems from other languages were translated by Vagaland. In *Ambrosia and Small Beer* Christopher Hassall quotes Edward Marsh's dictum on poetry translation that it is 'obvious that the only way to translate is to get a good grasp of the author's thought and feeling and then recast it according to the genius of one's own language' – a theory amply illustrated by Vagaland.

In October 1952, not long after our engagement, I spent a holiday in Shetland and we paid a visit to Weisdale, the birthplace of Vagaland's mother. The occasion was later to be fraught with distressful memories for us both, for the breakdown in my health which had been impending for some years occurred soon afterwards, and was serious and prolonged. No description of the anguish caused by this illness will be attempted here, but all the poems written at this time are evidence of undiminished love and constancy. One of them is 'Blugga Flooers':

> My tochts gengs back ta da sun-bricht mödow,
>   Whaar da burn rins doon be da blugga-flooers,
> Whaar we wid play, whin we wir bairns,
>   Trowe aa da lent o da sunny ooers.

---

truck a gaet – tramp a path.

Da blugga blossoms sweet in Simmer,
An da stripe still sings da sam aald sang,
Bit du's no here aside me, Yarta,
An a'm tinkin lang, oh, A'm tinkin lang.

I lift da lid o my kyist fast-stekkit,
An I gyoppen in till I fin my share
O da silver bricht o da rinnin water
An da blugga's gold at we gaddered dere.

My silver an gold'll keep me livin
Till dee an me eence mair sall meet;
Till I sall fin dee ida Simmer
Wi da blugga-flooers aroond dy feet.

It is not easy for me to dwell on the painful memories of my breakdown but I must do so long enough to introduce another poem written during this period:

Love o my Hert

Minds du da day at we göd ower ta Weisdale?
An foo we waandered ta dat quiet place
Whaar lang sin syne da Aamos Kirk wis biggit
An cöst aa roond da blissin o its paece.

An heard as we göd back alang da water,
Da laebrak lullin, low an musical –
Dat place whaar eence a Island king wis cradled
Among da trees, aside da Wissin Wal.

Below da trees, whaar saft, sweet rain wis faain,
Du liftit up dy face fir me ta kiss;
Fooever lang we wait fir een anidder,
Lord grant at, some day, we sall get wir wiss!

---

mödow – meadow; blugga-flooers – marsh marigolds; stripe – small stream; Yarta – loved one; tinkin lang – thinking with longing; fast-stekkit – tightly closed; gyoppen – lift with both hands.

---

laebrak – a long comber breaking against the shore; Wissin Wal – Wishing Well.

The ruins of the Aamos (Alms) Kirk, as also the birthplace of the 'Island King', are still to be seen in Weisdale. The 'Island King' featured in one of my strange coincidences, noted down on 30th June 1977.

'In attempting to catalogue my husband's books – a task which proceeds very fitfully – I find myself engrossed in reading parts of them. Two days ago, when consulting my medical dictionary, I noticed that the book alongside was *The Kings of the Cocos*, given by my sister, Vaila, to Alex some years ago. A sudden surge of interest made me sit down with this book, and after looking at a few pages I skimmed through the most of it, confirming what I already knew, that the birthplace of the first "King of the Cocos" is in Weisdale, Shetland.

'Peculiarly stirred by what I had read, I yesterday identified in my World Atlas the location of the Cocos Islands.

'This morning the radio news contains an item about the Cocos, "still governed by a Clunies-Ross, descendant of the original 'King'." The islands now belong to the Australian government who want to change the conditions of government by Clunies-Ross, who, however, claims that the inhabitants are perfectly happy and satisfied with the present regime.'

The fact that this book, *The Kings of the Cocos*, was alongside my medical dictionary on our bookshelves reminds me that the dictionary seems to have been the linking factor in another sequence of occurrences, noted on 2nd October 1976:

'Received a letter yesterday from a friend in Wales. He asked whether I had ever read *The Crystal Cave* by Mary Stewart. I recalled that Alex had read a whole series of Mary Stewart's books. I had read on or two myself, but not *The Crystal Cave*.

'First thing this morning I listened to a radio talk on farming in which an infection was discussed which was at one time also diagnosed in human beings. I decided to consult my medical book. It was in its usual place on the bookshelves. I wondered why it was placed here – were there other medical books alongside? No, but the first book to the left was *The Crystal Cave* by Mary Stewart! I had not realised that the book was in my possession. For months I have been concentrating on books of poetry at the other end of the bookshelves which line the wall of our sitting-room, and have also been making frequent visits to our local library to select anthologies, biographies, etc.

One of the most beautiful love poems in the Shetland dialect is surely 'Water Lilies', which first appeared, I see, in *The New Shetlander* of June 1950. This flower seems to have had an exceptional, even mystical, significance for Vagaland. As well as in this early poem, it features in one of his last, 'Flooer o da Licht'. Here is 'Water Lilies':

> Whin da laeves an buds o da water-lilies
>   Spread roond da loch dir dark-green frill
> I took my tushkar be Lungawater
>   An cöst a bank near Stoorbra Hill.
>
> Da hill laek a kummelled boat wis lyin,
>   Grown ower wi moss ida lang Jöne days,
> An white apo white da water-lilies,
>   Whin du cam dere wi me ta raise.
>
> Da stack wis beelt an da coarn gaddered
>   An dan I hed ta geng awa,
> Bit I tink o da lilies aft wi langer,
>   Noo everything is smoored in snaa.
>
> I think o dee be da oppen fire,
>   As du sits an looks at da golden glöd
> Laek gold ida cups o white water-lilies,
>   Whaar I drank sweetness afore I göd.

The poem refers to the successive stages by which peat is acquired for winter firing. The 'tushkar' is the peat-cutting implement. 'Ta raise' is 'to set up the peats to dry'. When brought home, they are built into a 'stack'. The scene is vivid, especially if one knows the area. The 'hill' is Stoorbra Hill, looking like 'a kummelled' (overturned) 'boat'. Lungawater is the name of the loch nearby where water lilies once grew in profusion but are probably less in evidence since the loch became a reservoir for the district's water supply.

---

cöst – p.p. of 'cast', to cut peats; to raise – to set up peats to dry; langer – longing; smoored – smothered; glöd – glow.

There is no doubt whence came the inspiration for the poem. Vagaland's brother, formerly a merchant seaman, was expert at 'casting peats', which involves cutting them and laying them on the peat bank in one deft manual operation! Formerly a very necessary skill in these northern isles.

One of Vagaland's early poems was inspired by fragments of old Norn, handed down orally and translated thus by Dr. Jakobsen when he visited Shetland at the beginning of the century: 'It is dark in the chimney, but it is light on the heath. There is still time for the guest to go.' Under the title 'Variation on an Old Theme', Norn and dialect combine to provide the music and rhythm of this unique love lyric:

> 'Myrkt er i ljora, myrkt er i ljora.'
> Sweet is dy lips, laek dew-weet smora.
> Dy folk wid stop wis, bit we'll come ower aa.
>
> 'Ljost er i lyngi, ljost er i lyngi.'
> Neist nicht i my boat ta my Isle A'll bring dee
> An safe as da shield-ring my airms'll ring dee.
>
> 'Timi at guestrinn, timi at guestrinn
> Gengri.' Noo da fools is nestin.
> Der a lang rodd afore me, an du sood be restin.

---

smora – clover; fools (Nor. *fugl*) – birds; rodd – road; sood – should.

Chapter 22

'He Prayeth Best . . .'

The 'peerie folk' who featured in the early poem "Nordern Lichts" had the following poem addressed to them after a journey in a friend's car on a dark winter night many years ago. Vivid memories remain of small, frightened, wild creatures, eyes bright in the car's headlights, scurrying for safety.

> Whin nicht draas da blinds doon, an lichts aa da starns,
>   Whin da day's toil is döne, and nae humans aboot
> Aless antrin een, makkin haem ida mirkenin,
>   Hit's dan at da Peerie Folk laeks ta be oot.
>
> Peerie Folk, Peerie Folk, whaar ir you come fae,
>   Oot o da hedder, fae hadds near an far?
> Look left an look richt here afore you start crossin,
>   Or you'll end up anunder da wheels o a car.
>
> Dey're plain ta be seen ida aze o da car-lichts –
>   A moose seekin shalter anunder a broo,
> A mismirised rabbit at's sittin sae gluffed-laek,
>   A hedgehug at's rowed himsell up in a clew.
>
> Peerie Folk, Peerie Folk, what ir you seekin,
>   Da neeps ida böl or da seed ida skroo?
> You'll be gyaain trowe da yaird-grinnds an aa roond da hooses
>   Ta see if der ony smaa morsel fir you.

---

antrin – occasional; gluffed – frightened; clew – ball (usually of wool); neeps – turnips; böl – container; skroo – corn-stack; grinnds – gates.

He Prayeth Best . . .

Da crops at's ingaddered, da coarn at's yaird-fastit
  Wi mony a sair rig, an wi mony a weet hide,
Is no fir wild craetirs; dey hardly need lippen
  Ta get mony inbös fae dem at's inside.

Peerie Folk, Peerie Folk, life is no aesy!
  Dis wirld ta begin wi wis med fir wis aa
(Sae we're telled) ida days o da Gairden o Eden,
  Bit noo hit's da poor at aye gengs ta da waa.

Noo man shörely tinks he's da Lord o Creation
  An ruler ower aathing at's doon here below.
He sood hae whin he can a smaa mizzer o mercy
  Or I warren at someday he'll get a firsmo.

Peerie Folk, Peerie Folk, blissin be wi you!
  May naebody grudge you your hermless fun;
If you tak, whin you're fantin, a grain o da baess-maet,
  Göd keep you aa safe fae da trap an da gun!

In 1973 a friend suggested that Vagaland should submit an entry for The World Wildlife Poetry Competition. Although by this time he was in rapidly deteriorating health, and struggling to complete preparation of the Shetland song book for the printers, he readily devoted his gifts to a cause dear to his heart.

Le Clameur de Haro

When winter storms are breaking o'er
The stacks and skerries by the shore,
And the great rocks from ocean's bed
  Are flung upon the strand,
The seal-folk journey where they please,
Regardless of the angry seas
  That lash the troubled land.

---

yaird-fastit – made secure; rig – back; hide – skin; lippen – expect; inbös – welcome; get a firsmo – get a rude awakening; baess-maet – animal fodder.

But when a breeze in Summer plays,
And when, in sultry, sunlit days,
Golden and bright, the Titbow Dance
   Is shimmering on the sea,
The wary seal-folk know full well
That they must have a sentinel
   To guard them faithfully.

If they should wish to leave the deep,
A little while on land to sleep,
They trust to have, not far away,
   A watcher in the sky;
One who will give, to keep their lives
Safe from the bullets and the knives,
   A timely, warning cry –

A friend, who is a friend indeed,
Will help wild creatures in their need,
As do the gulls who guard the seals
   Upon a beach below;
Will speak, or write, it well may be,
Or raise, in their extremity,
   A clamour of 'Haro!'

   The adjudicators commended the poem in these words: 'T. A. Robertson of the Shetlands has the truly poetical concept of threatened nature calling in aid "*Le Clameur de Haro*", the immediate cry for help anciently customary (and perhaps still heard occasionally) in the Channel Islands.'

   'The Titbow Dance' was one of the names in the Shetland dialect for the quivering light over the hills, or the dancing shimmer over the sea, in hot weather.

   It was an old belief in Shetland that a seal, before going to sleep, would get a gull to keep watch.

   I have already quoted the poem 'Widwick' in which our small Shetland sheepdog, 'Susie', featured. She appears again in 'Treasure', in which an elderly crofter soliloquises thus:

Da whalp he rins aboot da hoose,
   An blyde enyoch is he,
If he can finn some peerie thing
   At he can play him wi.

A bit o clod ta shaste aboot
　　Below a restin-shair;
Some paper rowed atil a baa
　　At he can showe an tear.

Bit sood you gie ta him a ben
　　Dan what a shange you see,
Fir aa his madrim an his fun
　　Is turned ta meesery.

He taks dat ben baith oot an in
　　An nearly faas a föl;
At last he hoids him in below
　　Da blanket in his böl.

An even dan he's no content –
　　he aye maan geng an look
Ta see if ony-een is taen
　　Da treasure fae his nyook.

Hit's jöst da sam wi mony a man –
　　Whin eence he's gaddered gair,
Dan he can tink o naethin else
　　Bit foo ta gadder mair.

Noo, if you hae baith maet an claes,
　　An somethin you can smok,
A grain o helt ta wirk your wark
　　Alang wi idder folk;

A haand ta help your neebor-man
　　Ta harl up life's brae,
A hert at keeps his livin fire –
　　Dat's aa you need ta hae.

There was no apparent reason why Susie chose to bury her bone under
the blanket in her basket, unless it was that the weather out of doors was at

---

whalp – young dog; clod – fragment of peat; restin-shair – settle; rowed – rolled; showe – chew; ben – bone; madrim – pranks; nearly faas a föl – nearly loses his reason; claes – clothes; helt – health; idder – other; harl – struggle.

times so boisterous. In the interests of hygiene the bone had, of course, to be removed, and her concern for her treasure was decidedly marked when possible thieves were around!

In *The Descent of Man* Darwin wrote: 'Dogs show what may be fairly called a sense of humour, as distinct from mere play; if a bit of stick or other such object be thrown to one, he will often carry it away for a short distance; and then, squatting down with it on the ground close before him, will wait until his master comes quite close to take it away. The dog will then seize it and rush away in triumph, repeating the same manoeuvre, and evidently enjoying the practical joke.' Our little dog had this sense of fun to the highest degree, and she was allowed to indulge it whenever possible!

I find it incomprehensible that anyone who has owned a dog and had its complete trust and affection should be in favour of vivisection. Is it generally known that Darwin also had something to say about this? Again in *The Descent of Man*, after quoting the sentence by 'an old writer' - 'A dog is the only thing on this earth that luvs you more than he luvs himself', he went on: 'In the agony of death a dog has been known to caress his master, and everyone has heard of the dog suffering under vivisection who licked the hand of the operator; this man, unless the operation was fully justified by an increase in our knowledge, or unless he had a heart of stone, must have felt remorse to the last hour of his life.' But can any and every action really be justified simply because it is done in the pursuit of knowledge?

A few years ago I read in *A Short History of Biology*, by Isaac Asimov, that in 1870 two German neurologists 'exposed the brain of a living dog and stimulated various portions with an electric needle'. The nineteenth century, with its widely introduced theory of evolution, seems to have seen the introduction also of the theory that man's intellect, used coldly in the pursuit of knowledge, must reign supreme over any feelings of sympathy and love.

Man's brain is said to have increased three times in size in the past 100,000 years. Another view is that it was formerly two-thirds of its present size. One does not hear whether the brain of the lower animal – ape, monkey, dog, etc. – has similarly increased in size. But here is what Darwin wrote in *The Descent of Man*:

> 'To maintain, independently of any direct evidence, that no animal during the course of ages has progressed in intellect or other mental faculties, is to beg the question of the evolution of species. We have seen that, according to Lartet, existing mammals belonging to several orders have larger brains than their ancient tertiary proto-types.'

The conclusion reached by Professor W. H. Thorpe in *Purpose in a World of Chance* was, I believe, that 'characters acquired by populations are inherited by their offspring populations if they are adaptive'.

Although, until comparatively recently at least, the increase in size of man's skull in the past 100,000 years has been regarded as indicative of an increase in intellect, Darwin as far back as 1871 did not seem to be wholly convinced. Again in *The Descent of Man* he wrote:

'... no one supposes that the intellect of any two animals or of any two men can be accurately gauged by the cubic content of their skulls. It is certain that there may be extraordinary mental activity with an extremely small absolute mass of nervous matter. Thus the wonderfully diversified instincts, mental powers and affections of ants are notorious, yet their cerebral ganglia are not so large as the quarter of a small pin's head. Under this point of view, the brain of an ant is one of the most marvellous atoms of matter in the world, perhaps more so than the brain of a man.'

If, as Darwin believed, there is no *fundamental* difference between man and the higher mammals in their mental faculties, is man entitled to take advantage simply because he has what he considers to be such a highly developed intellect?

Animals and birds were the subject of a number of Vagaland's poems. In the dialect poem 'Da Otter an Da Hedgehug' the animals exchange philosophies in what A. D. Mackie, in a review of *Mair Laeves*, aptly described as 'a La Fontaine conversation'!

Da Otter an Da Hedgehug

Da streen as da Dim begöd ta turn,
A Otter cam ta da mooth o da burn;
An a Hedgehug sittin apo da brig
Lookit doon wi his ee sae glig.
'Fine nicht,' said da Otter.
   'He's truly dat,'
Da Hedgehug answered, 'An weel I wat
He'll be a fine day da moarn tö,

Dim (Simmer Dim) – time between sunset and sunrise when it is never quite dark; begöd – began; glig – observant.

If da wind gengs Wast, as he's shöre ta dö.
Whin da sun gengs doon in a bank, ye see,
Dan da wind is shöre ta be Wasterly.'
'Ya, dat's ower true.'
'Noo, Dratsie, boy,
Keep oot o da ee o da brig, my joy.
At dayset I skuttit trowe a slap,
An I saa a man dere settin a trap.
If du gengs in yunder, dy maen is med.'
'Noo da Loard bliss dee,' da Otter said,
'A freend ida wye is better ta hae
As a penny ita da purse, dey say.'
'Ya,' said da Hedgehug, 'Ye böst ta try
An obleege a freend, whatever wye;
Bit foo is du bön livin aa year?
Hit's a lang while noo fae I saa dee here.'
'Weel,' said da Otter, 'I canna complain,
If onlie folk wid lat me alane.
At times A'm faered at I micht be shot
Ta mak some wife a furry cott.
An dan I winder at da greed
O dem wi mair as what dey need.
No at I grudge dem siller, A'm shöre,
If dey wid bear an haal wi da pör.
Ye can mak a livin, gyaain ta da sea,
Bit da fishin is no what hit ösed ta be.
Der a lok ta pit up wi, as I could tell –
Bit foo is du bön keepin dysell?'
'Weel,' said da Hedgehug, 'I try my best
Ta cloor fir a livin alang wi da rest.
I varg aboot ida eart nae want,
Bit sometimes, truly, A'm laek ta fant;
An folks gets as tirn as dey can be,
An wid tak me an höve me apo da sea,
Fir dey say at I tak da eggs fae da nest
An sook da coo, whin shö's haein a rest.'

---

dratsie – otter; slap – an opening in a dyke; skutted – peeped; dy maen is med – your fate is sealed; bear an haal wi – sympathise with and help; cloor – scrape; fant – starve with hunger; höve – heave.

'An dös du?'
'Weel, Dratsie, I sanna lee,
An Göd firgie me, fir A'm no free
O takkin a antrin egg or twa;
I kyin ower weel hit's against da laa,
Bit him at judges me canna tell
What he micht be pitten til himsell.'
'Ower true,' said da Otter, 'Da wye at hit is
Hit's a poor ootlook fir da laeks o wis,
An, if you traivel, whatever da place,
Da wan thing you never can fin is paece.'
Sae he said, an da Hedgehug answered him,
'Der mony a shange in a Simmer Dim.
Lat alane in a Winter's nicht.
Some day da wirld'll be pitten richt.'
Dey sat an spak, an firyat da time,
As A'm set doon i dis bit o rhyme,
Till apo da hill da new-boarn day
Aa rosy an bricht wi promise lay,
An his waarm fingers touched da grund
As da sun was risin abön da Pund.

In 1975 I began to read all I could about the theory of evolution, and how man (and all animated being?) was believed to have evolved from a single cell, an amoeba. One sunny day in June of that year I sat with a friend on a hillside in the country, while her husband set off to photograph wild birds. The subject of evolution was uppermost in my mind and I talked for some time, no doubt boringly, about this remarkable single cell, the amoeba.

Next day, while sewing, I found myself watching casually the TV programme *Star Trek*, a rare occurrence for me. In this particular episode the space ship encountered a giant amoeba, 1,000 miles across!

Another coincidence, connected with bats (which have presumably evolved like the rest of us from an amoeba!) may appropriately be related here.

'On 8th December 1976, when I switched on the radio early in the morning, I heard a reference to the belief that bats could become

---

firgie – forgive; antrin – occasional; firyat – forgot; Pund – enclosure.

entangled in a woman's hair. The speaker said this had never been known to happen. I thought about this for a while and, in my ignorance, decided that bats must have eyes that can see in the dark.

'On my way home I called along the local library, as I was at that time looking for books on genetics. A book called *Mysterious Senses* caught my eye. I opened it at random and there on the open page was a drawing of a bat, and on the page opposite, under the heading "Ears that see", the words: "It has been known since the 'forties' that they (bats) utter ultrasonic sounds inaudible to the human ear, and use the echoes to locate obstacles, or their prey . . . The lesser horseshoe bat can 'see' with its ultrasonic ears better than a human eye can see by day."'

Chapter 23

Eence Apon a Time . . .

In company Vagaland was reserved to a degree which many people mistook for extreme shyness. His contribution to any conversation was usually the result of careful consideration, and was often given only when asked for. More than once he told me that he had no gift for 'small talk', an area in which I fear he may have considered me more than proficient! And he had the uncanny gift of detaching himself from deep concentrated thought and recovering the trend of a question or remark made by me a few minutes earlier. My challenges on such occasions provided us both with great amusement.

His humour was quiet and deliberate, and because of its unexpectedness was all the more effective. In particular, it found expression when he wrote for children's entertainment. I do not know where the following nursery tale may have originated, possibly in Norway, but it is one told by my husband:

> 'Eence apon a time dey wir tree princes. Da name o da first een wis SKRATT. Da name o da second een wis SKRATT-SKRATTERAT, an da name o da third een wis SKRATT-SKRATTERAT-SKRAT-SKRUIN-SKRAT.
> 'At da sam time dey wir tree princesses. Da name o da first een wis SIPP. Da name o da second een wis SIPP-SIPPENIP, an da name o da third een wis SIPP-SIPPENIP-SIP-SUREN-SIP.
> 'Dey aa grew up tagyidder an SKRATT mairried SIPP, SKRATT-SKRATTERAT mairried SIPP-SIPPENIP, and SKRATT-SKRATTERAT-SKRAT-SKRUIN-SKRAT mairried SIPP-SIPPENIP-SIP-SUREN-SIP, an dey aa lived happily ever eftir.'

My wider reading in recent years has included a number of biographies. I was particularly fascinated by Christopher Hassall's biography of Rupert Brooke, and remember clearly a 'coincidence' connected with it.

The book describes the production of Milton's *Comus* by Rupert Brooke and his fellow students at Cambridge University. Among the helpers and designers who were described were Gwen Darwin (granddaughter of Darwin) who later became Gwen Raverat, and another fellow student, Sybil Pye. Next morning, after reading this, I tidied some old papers and magazines which had been preserved by my husband, and decided to keep a catalogue entitled 'The One Hundred Best Books for Children' – a *Sunday Times* survey. On opening it, the title 'Red-Letter Holiday' caught my eye. It was the title of a book by Virginia Pye, with illustrations by Gwen Raverat! Here I have to reveal my ignorance and confess that before reading the biography I did not even know that such people had existed.

I kept the catalogue of children's books for good and sentimental reasons, for it reminded me how much in his capacity as teacher, my husband had the interests of the schoolchildren at heart. Those whom he taught were generally in the age group of twelve to fifteen or sixteen years. What was probably the most characteristic thing about him, however, was that he appealed especially to the very young and the very old. His depth of experience of life's hardships and trials gave him, I think, a certain affinity with the old, and yet at the same time he never lost his affinity with the child mind, amply demonstrated in his Bairn-Rhymes. One of these is 'Da Cat an da Moose':

>Da cat lay afore da fire
> Sleepin, sleepin.
>Oot cam a peerie moose,
> Creepin, creepin.
>
>Da cat waakened up an sat
> Blinkin, blinkin.
>Dere wis a peerie moose
> Slinkin, slinkin.
>
>'Noo, my fine jantleman,
> Tell me, tell me,
>What du's come oot ta stael –
> Spaek, or A'll fell dee!'

'Plaese, Mester Purriman,
 Dönna be tirn;
 Lat me win oot o here
 Roond be da kirn.'

'Whaar, tinks du, wid du geng?
 Faase tief, A'll watch dee!
 Du'll no win back nae mair,
 Dis time A'll catch dee.'

'Weel, I wis gyaan ta see
 Some o my bridders,
 Sisters, an cöshins tö,
 An twartree idders.

'A'll maybe bid dem come
 Back fir a banket
 Fir der nae want o maet
 Here, Göd be tankit.'

'Tell me, my boannie laad,
 What gaet du'll traivel.'
'Doon trowe da peerie höl
 Dere ida gaevel.'

'Bid dy freends, I sall be
 Ower blyde ta see dem.
 Haest dee! I trust dey'll bring
 Aa dir kin wi dem.'

Da cat sat afore da fire,
 Blinkin, blinkin,
Da moose he göd doon da höl,
 Linkin, linkin.

Perhaps, however, the most popular 'bairn-rhyme', familiar to both young and old alike, is 'Santie's Reindeer' which first appeared in *The New Shetlander* Christmas number, 1951, in a full page setting, with surrounding illustrations by our local artist, Frank Walterson. Twenty-five

---

kirn – churn; cöshins – cousins; banket – banquet; göd – went; linkin – running very fast.

years later it appeared in the form of a Christmas card, in aid of charity, and found its way, I am told, to the far corners of the world.

> Da Göd Man hings da starns oot
>   Laek peerie lamps sae bricht,
> Sae Santie Klaas can fin his wye,
>   Whin he comes here da nicht.
>
> Dis nicht he yoks his reindeer up,
>   An drives dem trowe da sky;
> Dan he taks on his muckle bag
>   An laeves his slaidge ootbye.
>
> An, Maamie, whin you mylk da coo
>   You'll geng an tak a skurt
> O hey, or maybe twartree shaeves
>   An laeve dem lyin furt.
>
> Da reindeer haes sae far ta geng;
>   Dey're maybe hed nae maet,
> An he'll be blyde if he can fin
>   A grain fir dem ta aet.
>
> A'll hing my sock apo da raep
>   Jöst in below da brace,
> An whin he's trivelled trowe da lum
>   He'll aesy fin da place.
>
> He'll never come till A'm asleep,
>   Sae A'll pit on my goon
> An up da stairs ita da laft
>   A'll geng an lay me doon.
>
> You'll pit da claes aboot me noo,
>   Becaase he's gittin late;
> An Maamie, whin you mylk da coo,
>   You'll mind da reindeer's maet.

---

starns – stars; fin – find; yoks – yokes; trowe – through; muckle – large; slaidge – sledge; skurt – armful; shaeves – sheaves; furt – outside; blyde – glad; raep – line above fire on which things are dried; brace – mantelpiece; trivel – feel one's way; lum – chimney; laft – loft; claes – clothes; maet – meat, food.

Notice that the respectful form of the pronoun is used by the child when addressing his mother, and not the familiar 'du'. This distinction is, of course, still preserved in many languages.

An old friend, Mima Arthurson (a gifted teacher before her marriage during the Second World War), when approaching her ninety-first birthday, revealed to me that the poem 'Santie's Reindeer' evoked such memories for her that she frequently regretted that she had never made it the subject of a talk. Knowing her abilities, I tentatively suggested that it might not be too late for her to commit her thoughts to writing. Here is her immediate response, with full permission to include it in my book if ever published.

19th August 1981

An imaginary talk given to a group of Shetlanders old enough to remember a Shetland cottage interior as it was when heated by a peat fire in a big chimney.

Santie's Reindeer

'You ask me why such an old person chose a children's poem as favourite. The reason is that I found the poet's heart in it. I feel that as a boy he felt grieved for animals who were hungry and would have given them what they needed. And when he grew to manhood he still kept those feelings as this delightful poem shows. I knew a young schoolboy who felt exactly as the boy in the poem, who asked his mother to lay outside some hay or sheaves "for dey're maybe hed nae maet, and he'll be blyde if he can fin a grain for dem ta aet".

'Can you see the lovely picture this poem draws for us? I can see it clearly. If you knew the living-room in a Shetland cottage in the days when a good peat-fire warmed it – when the plain white wood furniture was scrubbed and pure white – the dresser with its drawers and cupboards, a resting-chair on which a man could lie at full length at one side of the fireplace, a chair at the other side on which the housewife sat knitting busily, a lamp hanging from a hook in the ceiling giving a soft light to the whole room, and on this particular Christmas eve a boy sitting on the resting-chair holding a favourite gift in his hand, his book and some cards fallen from his seat unheeded. He was not really playing with his toy. He was thinking deeply, and his face wore a look of worry even for one so young. It was late in the evening, the time for the animals who were in the byre to be fed, and if a cow had milk the housewife would bring in that grand fresh milk which the family would enjoy at next morning's breakfast. So her thoughtful boy asks her to lay outside some hay or maybe "twartree shaeves" for the reindeer who had come so far on this cold night. If I am not mistaken, she expected him to ask for that, and he would expect her to lay the food down in a clean, dry place in the shelter of the house. Santa would come near to the house before he pulled the reins to stop his sledge, and, old as he was, he never had trouble in reaching the chimney and finding the place where the socks were hung – "juist in below da brace". His muckle bag was filled with packets addressed to boys and girls, and his pockets held oranges and apples, and maybe also a few bright shining shillings and sixpenny pieces to put into the toes of socks. He always knew where to find the right boys and girls and where to leave his sledge while he nimbly performed his Christmas eve duty.

'While the mother prepares to go to the barn and byre the boy decides to go to bed "for he'll never come till A'm asleep . . . an, Maamie, whin you milk da coo, you'll mind da reindeer's maet". He did not forget to hang up his sock and he expected his old friend, Santa, but food for the hungry animals was his deepest thought, and he would carry that kind feeling always as he grew. He had gifts of mind and body, but these spiritual gifts had been generously bestowed on him, and he would nourish them as he grew. Shetland, and especially our old "toon" are the poorer now that our gifted poet Vagaland has passed from us, but I like to think that some of the many boys he taught have been influenced enough by him to remember him with love and to foster those gifts in themselves – if so, Vagaland will not have lived in vain. And now he has received the reward of a life well-lived and we must not mourn his passing.'

Chapter 24

Viking Voyagers

The imagination of many people, but particularly those who live in the Northern hemisphere, must have been stirred by the presentation of the television series *The Vikings*, with Magnus Magnusson as narrator.

The eighth number of the series dealt with the Norse discovery of America and located those areas where evidence had been found of Viking settlements. Of particular interest to me was the one at L'Anse aux Meadows in Newfoundland, identified by Dr. Helge Ingstad as a Norse settlement dating from around the year 1000.

My husband's interest in this site was aroused by press cuttings about the 'find', sent to him by his friend Professor Isachsen, of the Geography Department of the University of Oslo, and his imagination was fired to the extent that his poem *'L'Anse aux Meadows'* appeared in the December 1971 number of *The New Shetlander*. Vagaland took pride in his Norse ancestry (as also his Scottish) and, as the poem shows, he thrilled to tales of courage and deeds of exploration.

> A'm seen da bricht mön sheenin laek a lantern ida evenin,
>   Seen da new mön wi da aald een in her lap,
> Bit ere-da-streen I saa her as I lookit trowe da lömer
>   Black an golden-yallow flekkit laek a map;
>   Markit jöst laek what you see apon a map.

---

ere-da-streen – the night before last; lömer – roof-light; flekkit – flecked or spotted.

An I tocht, der mony a hidden thing benon da cloods o Heevin,
  An mony a thing at nane can understaand,
Bit noo I kyin for certain at athin yun sheenin circle
  What A'm lookin at is jöst anidder laand,
  Naethin idder bit a far-aff uncan laand.

An I tocht aboot da twa brave men at first set fit apon her
  An dat idder een atil a crew o tree,
Vaigin jöst da wye at Veekings fae dir hadds ita da Norlaand
  Eence göd vaigin an explorin ower da sea;
  Sailin oot fae Norwa ower da Western Sea.

Rowin, sailin, ower da Swan's Path an awa apo da Ocean,
  Vaigin far an farder wast across da faem.
Some o dem göd on fae Faera till dey wan as far as Iceland,
  Dey wir idders at in Greenland med a haem;
  Ya, Red Erik's men in Greenland med dir haem.

Hit wis dere dey heard a römer o a place at wis bön sichtit
  Ta da Wastird, maybe tree days' sail awa,
An Leif Eriksson wis aaber fir ta see if dey could finn it;
  What dey fann at first wis maistly rocks an snaa;
  Stennie beaches, muckle hills aa smoored wi snaa.

Bit dey vaiged still farder sooth doon by a shore wi lang, white beaches,
  Till dey cam apon a place baith green an fair,
Bricht wi flooers ita da mödows, ower da knowes da mist-blue berries;
  Dey wir truly braaly tankfil ta be dere;
  Dey wir blyde at dey wir med a laandfaa dere.

Fir dat place hed maistly aa-thing at a boddie could a needit;
  Dey wir girse enyoch ta feed baith sheep an kye,
Loks o trees whaar dey could get da wid ta beeld dir boats an hooses,
  Göd black iron fir da sem an röve firbye;
  An a fouth o fish ita da sea firbye.

---

benon – beyond; tree – three; vaigin – voyaging; hadds – (here, settlements); römer – rumour; aaber – eager; sem – kind of nails used in making a clinker-built boat; sem an röve – nails and washers used in rivetting as above; fouth – large quantity.

An I tocht aboot Columbus tö, whin he set oot fae Palos,
   Tinkin he wid mak a landfaa in Cathay,
Bit he fann a place wi things at folk in Europe never dremt o
   Whin he laandit in San Salvador ee day;
   An da Aald Wirld an da New een met dat day.

Nae man kyins what may happen whin da rocket-ships is sailin
   Far awa among da starns we see abön;
Bit we're seen men gyaain back an fore, an heard whit dey wir sayin
   Among da rocks an craters o da mön;
   Whin dey laandit at da Mountains o da Mön.

Whin da folk apo dis planet starts ta winder what's aroond dem,
   Dan der wan thing shöre – o dat I hae nae doot;
Nae maitter foo dey sheeks an spaek an traep wi een anidder,
   Foo hit aa began dey never will finn oot;
   Whaar hit cam fae, dat dey never will finn oot.

Awa in Göd's grit Universe, among da mirds o starns,
   Hit's hard ta say what windros things may be;
Wi dir telescopes an space-probes folk can learn a grain aboot it,
   Bit a better thing ta dö is geng an see;
   Laek Leif Eriksson, dey'll better geng an see!

   I do not suppose that General Stafford, who spoke on 19th October 1981 in the radio programme *Start the Week with Richard Baker* about the three astronauts involved in the first moon landing, is aware that Collins, the third member of the crew, who had to remain on board the spaceship, is commemorated, along with the two astronauts who actually landed on the moon, in this (see third verse) and other Vagaland poems.
   How is the following kind of experience to be accounted for? On 9th July 1975, in a reference on radio to the discovery of America by Columbus in 1492, the speaker added that there were, of course, claims that the continent had been discovered earlier by others; for example, the Vikings. This led me to look, without success, in our bookshelves for information about the landing by Leif Eriksson circa 1000. On 10th July, the following morning, Richard Baker included, in his radio programme *These you have Loved*, a song about the bluebird, which he said had often

---

sheeks – talks excessively; traep – argue; mirds – multitudes; starns – stars.

been requested. This recalled to me that, shortly before he died, my husband had attempted to write a poem about the bluebird, and I was led to consult the notebook which contained his last entries. Tied up with the notebook and other papers, I noticed a booklet entitled *The Norsemen in America*, and in this I found the information about Leif Eriksson for which I had been looking the previous day!

Since Viking times at least, and until only recently, Shetland has produced a race of seafarers, for the obvious reason that the islanders depended largely on the harvest of the sea for survival. This fact emphasises the dangers of the present threat to her fishing industry, and the growth of a generation of young men attracted, understandably, to more rewarding occupations connected with the oil industry. There is a danger, if the situation continues, that what were formerly innate skills of seamanship may gradually be lost. In the past the skill and courage of Shetland's sea-going men has been known worldwide, and in the not so distant past, during the Napoleonic wars, the Royal Navy made relentless efforts to 'press' them into service.

Fishing about a century ago, in the often tempestuous seas surrounding the islands, undoubtedly demanded great courage. The hazards of 'haaf' (deep sea) fishing, in six-oared open boats, hardly need to be described. Force ten, or more, gales, which can spring up so suddenly around these coasts, have caused major disasters, still fresh in memory, in which fathers, sons and brothers lost their lives.

What was known last century as the 'Faeroe Fishin' – the title of one of Vagaland's poems – was conducted in boats known as 'smacks'. The exploits of those sailing from the West side of Shetland to Faeroe are described in the book *Rough Island Story* – long out of print – by William Moffatt, one of Shetland's sons who settled in Leeds.

That their seamanship has always been in great demand is further demonstrated by the fact that, from early last century until about the middle of the present one, large numbers of Shetland men took part in the whaling expeditions to South Georgia, involving prolonged absence from home throughout the long winter months, and into the late Spring.

Doubtless the greatest hardships experienced by the islanders were those brought about by the 'clearances', mostly in the first half of the nineteenth century, which deprived crofters of their fertile land and obliged them to move to more barren areas, even to outlying islands. With large families to support, and faced with inadequate means of survival, many opted to emigrate, mainly to New Zealand and Australia. The *Olearia*, or Australian Daisy Bush, which now thrives in parts of Shetland, inspired this poem by Vagaland:

At Simmer's end da hey is coled
An coarn starts ta turn ta gold,
An gairden flooers is lowin red
Afore da time at dey maan fade.

Among da flooers an trees der een,
Whin Simmer-time is nearly geen,
At staands, green-cled an fair ta see,
Mylk-white in aa her finery.
Shö dösna come fae near at haand,
Bit fae a far-aff Suddern laand,
At lies ita da sunsheen's aze
(Whin we hae Winter's mirkenin days),
Wi coral rocks, an waarm seas,
(Whin here-aboot we're laek ta freeze).

An hit's a laand at's aalwis dear
Ta mony a een at's geen fae here,
Yet still haes memories o haem –
Da Aald Rock ida Wastern faem,
Da Winter sea, sae faerce an grim,
Da glory o da Simmer Dim,
White cloods across da moarnin-blue,
An kokkiluries bricht wi dew.

An sae da Daisy-bush, I tink,
Fir Shetland folk is wan mair link
Atil a shain aroond da Eart
At joins twa places far apairt.
Half-wye across da wirld, we kyin,
Der mony o wir clossest kin;
Da Suddern Cross is sheenin doon
Ower lonlie station, croodit toon,
An, ower a Continent, a lok
O blöd-freends ta da Shetlan folk.

---

coled – gathered into haycocks; coarn – oats; lowin – flaming; aze – brilliance; mirkenin –
darkening; moarnin – morning; kokkiluries – daisies; shain – chain; croodit toon – crowded
town.

Night-Scented Stock in Bloom?

An whin dir fore-bears left da Isles
Ta vaige fir seeven thoosand miles,
We trust at, i dir herts, dey took
Across da sea ta mony a nyook
Da best-wirt things at can be named –
Kindness alaek ta sib an fremmed,
Help til a neebor in his need,
Things o da hert ta growe laek seed
Aa trowe dat laand across da sea,
An flooer fir lang in liberty.

---

sib – kinsman; fremmed – stranger.

Chapter 25
Disbelief Suspended!

Clear midnight comes to dwellings by the shore-line,
And through the hills there is so little sound
That you may think you hear the dwarfs of Gaemmla
At work within their caverns underground.
                                        (Vagaland)

These four lines from the poem 'Simmer Dim' came forcibly to mind as I watched the opening scenes from Wagner's opera *The Ring* relayed on television from Bayreuth.

Folk tales and legends are preserved in much of Shetland's recent literature – such as the Folk Books published by The Shetland Folk Society, Ernest Marwick's *Folk Tales of Orkney and Shetland* (1975), and more recently Jim Nicolson's *Shetland Folklore*. But numerous writers during the past century, whose books are out of print, have made their valuable contribution.

Some of these legends are handled with skill and imagination in Vagaland's poetry. 'Fae da Grund', for anyone like myself who grew up in a countryside surrounded by lonely hills, does have an aura of probability?

As I cam by da Trölligirts
An stoppit at da Millburn broo,
I met a peerie osmil wife
An shö wis gadderin lukkie's oo.

Trölligirts – a place-name in Waas, Shetland, meaning the home of the trolls; broo – brow or bank; peerie – small; osmil – sinister-looking; lukkie's oo – wild cotton.

'Göd wife, ye're trang,' I said ta her.
    Shö held up some fir me ta see.
'A'll caird it on my cairds o green,
    An spin, an mak a sark fir dee.

'An whin du slips him ower dy head,
    Du'll see what nane is seen fir lang;
Du'll kyin da Nyugl by da burn,
    Du'll listen ta da Filgee's[1] sang.

'Da doors, in green knowes oppenin,
    Will lukk dee in among wis aa,
An dere, whaar time gengs dancin by,
    Du'll never want ta win awa.'

'Nae need ta spaek o dat da day,
    Da sark is nedder med or skoored.'
Wi dat I spanged across da burn
    An left her, as shö stöd an glooered.

I göd a stramp or twa up ower
    An turned ta fin mysell alane,
An naethin by da burn ava
    Bit a grey, crookit, staandin-sten.

Myths and legends, or stories dealing with the supernatural, have, I must confess, never for the greater part of my long life made a strong appeal to me, but experiences in recent years have certainly caused me to question my innate tendency to rationalize everything! It happens that the two 'coincidences' which I now relate are concerned with stories which make a demand on the imagination.

'(13.1.76) Before bedtime last night I read a little from Tolkien's *The Hobbit* and reached the part where hobbit and dwarves were trapped in the Goblin's Cave, where the Wizard killed some of

---

[1] 'The Filgee' was an invisible being whose song foreboded death, not to the person who heard it, but to anyone who was with him or her at the time.

---

trang – busy; caird – card; Nyugl – water horse; skoored – washed; spanged – leapt; glooered – glowered; stramp – stride.

them with a magic flaming sword. This morning I switched on the radio and heard about Odysseus and his men trapped in a cave with the one-eyed Cyclops, and how Odysseus blinded the giant with the fiery brand!
'(11.10.76) After wondering this morning about the miracles of Christ, which mere reason is unable to accept, I later turned to my reading for today, to find these words: "Let us not try to eliminate the supernatural and bring it down to the plane of our own reason and knowledge; . . ."'

My note for the same day continues:

'Also, having heard early this morning on radio a conversation about a new translation of the Bible, called *The Good News Bible* being published today, it seemed remarkable that the Bible reading referred to should continue thus: "Let us translate every word of it [the Bible] into our lives. Let us each be a new edition and a new version of the scriptures . . ."'

Folk tales about seal folk are common to most islands and many are preserved in Orkney and Shetland. It seems that seal folk never regarded their stay on land as more than temporary, and, like ourselves, or most of us, could not deny the longing to return to native haunts and early associations. Often they left behind a heartbroken partner, with a plaint such as is voiced in 'Da Selkie Wife':

> Da sea is flat-calm; der nae brak ower da skerries.
>   Sae wis it eence, lang sin syne,
> Whin I fan dee, my love, at da first o da daylicht,
>   An aksed dee if du wid be mine.
> Dere du wis sittin, my boannie sea-maiden,
>   Doon by a sten at da ayre,
> Dy peerie feet bare, an dy selskyin aside dee,
>   An reddin dy golden hair.
>
> Simmer seas roond da Vee Skerries
>   Simmer dance ower da sea.
> Du left da haem o da Sel-folk,
>   Left it an cam ta me.

---

brak – break; sten – (here) rock; selskyin – sealskin; reddin – combing.

Night-Scented Stock in Bloom?

Bit, lass, der a shange ida dead o da Winter,
    Da frost, an da caavie o snaa.
An aa-man is aaber ta seek, whin he mirkens,
    Da shalter o röf-tree an waa.
An happy wir we, in wir ain hoose tagyidder,
    Mony a Winter-nicht lang,
As du sat at dy wheel ida aze o da firelicht,
    Singin a saft sleepy-sang.

Brakkin seas ida sea-helyer,
    Brimmastyooch ower da sea.
Waitin here, A'm hert-brokken.
    Comes du nae mair ta me?

Du widna a left me, my hert tells me truly,
    Fir aa at du langed fir da sea,
If it hedna a bön fir da selkie-folk's doin –
    Dey cöst sic a greest apo dee.
Dan du slippit awa, wi dy selskyin aboot dee,
    An doon at da ayre du göd in,
An du followed dem back trowe da caves o da ocean
    Til a place at I never could fin.

Far awa ower da wide water,
    Back ta da Sea-folk's place;
Hert o mine, du's lang-lippened –
    Whan will I see dy face?

---

caavie – snowstorm; aaber – eager; mirkens – darkens; röf-tree – roof (wooden); helyer – cave; brimmastyooch – spindrift; greest – spell.

Chapter 26

Lyric Poet

'For more than two thousand years the distinguishing
characteristic of poetry has been the element of song'
(Alfred Noyes – *Two Worlds for Memory*)

In the Shetland songbook 'Da Sangs at A'll Sing ta Dee', edited by T. A. Robertson, and published by The Shetland Folk Society in 1973, a few Vagaland songs are included. Notes on the songs are provided, and I find these remarks against 'Shetlan Gairden': 'The beauty of the many-coloured wild flowers is more noticeable because trees are few in number. The words were set to music by Shirley Peterson when she was only five years old.'

>   My gairden rins for seeventy miles
>   Fae Soombra Head ta Skaw;
>   Der no a brig fae isle ta isle,
>   Der no a gairden waa;
>
>   Bit aa da wye fae Sooth ta Nort,
>   Fae Aest ta Wast fir miles
>   Ye'll fin da wild flooers growin ta mak
>   A gairden o da Isles.
>
>   Da wild, free winds fae every ert
>   Blaas in across da sea;
>   Da flooers maan kroag as best dey can,
>   Der very little lee.

---

brig – bridge; ert – direction; kroag – shelter.

Hoidin among da short hill girse
   Is mony a peerie moot;
An yallow-gold, an pink an white,
   Ye see dem peepin oot.

Alang da side o every burn,
   Anunder every broo,
Dey're here and dere, a joy ta see –
   Mylk-white, an maave, an blue.

Dey're wuppled roond da maain-girse
   In mödows growin green,
An safe fae wind, becaase da tane
   Hadds up da tidder een.

Tae-girse alang da Spiggie Rodd,
   Da hedder-hills in Waas,
Da Blok-flooers up be Mavins Grinnd –
   A'll say nae mair, becaase

In every place fae Sooth ta Nort
   Fae Aest ta Wast fir miles,
Ye'll fin da wild flooers growin ta mak
   A gairden o da Isles.

'Lullaby ida Mirkenin', an early lyric, reveals a compassion which identifies completely with the situation it describes. A translation from the Norwegian of Nordahl Grieg, it was set to music by Ronnie Mathewson, an accomplished Shetland musician and composer.

   Nicht ita da Nort is lang;
   Maamie sings a sleepy-sang.
   Caald he mirkens ower da sea;
   Peerie licht – come ta me.

---

girse – grass; wuppled – twined; maain-girse – grass for cutting; mödows – meadows; da tane . . . da tidder – the one . . . the other; Tae-girse – thyme; hedder – heather; Blok-flooers – marsh marigolds.

Mirkenin – the gloaming; mirkens – darkens.

Caald-rife wis da day at's geen;
Sheenin blue dy boannie een
Laek da flooer closin noo;
Peerie licht – sleep du.

Moarnin brings nae sun-blink here,
Nane ava bit dee, my dear.
By nane bit dee my hert is aesed;
Peerie licht – waaken plaesed!

Vagaland's mother, widowed when he was only one year old, certainly knew something of the deep underlying sadness at the heart of this lullaby, and for Vagaland himself I have no doubt that the original poem by Nordahl Grieg revived childhood memories.

'Lullaby ida Mirkenin' appeared in *Laeves fae Vagaland*, a first collection of poems published in 1952. By way of contrast, 'Lullaby fir Rachel', written in later years, is in much happier vein, with its prospect of family 'togetherness' at the end of the Voar (Spring) day's work:

Hushie-baa, my peerie jewel,
Hushie-baa, my dear.
Ower da hill da licht is dim
An sleepy time is near.

Noo da peerie dug is sittin
Lookin at da door,
Lippenin at da folk'll come –
Dat's what he dös in Voar.

Shön dey'll be a starn sheenin
Trowe da window-peen.
Shön dey'll gadder up abön,
Da starns een be een.

Een fir Faider, een fir Midder,
Een fir Meryn tö,
Een fir Aandroo, een fir Dy,
Dat's five, an dat'll dö.

---

caald-rife – very cold; peerie – little.

Lippenin – expecting; dey'll (Nor. *det vil*) – there will; window-peen – window-pane; Dy – Granpa.

Whin da folk can see five starns
   Sheenin ida lift
Dan dey'll kyin da time is come
   Ta end da Voar day's trift.

Hushie-baa, my peerie jewel,
   Hushie-baa, my dear.
Aa da folk is comin haem,
   An sleepy time is near.

As mentioned elsewhere, several of Vagaland's lyrics have been provided with music by different local composers, not least among whom is Shetland's songster, Shirley Peterson, who, along with her father, Larry, has broadcast on several occasions on radio and television. A number of readers will be familiar with her recording, at the tender age of six, of 'Da Rabbit's Lullaby'. This was a lullaby not just for any pet rabbit but for the one the poet had seen her nursing!

Hushie-baa, Fluffy,
   hushie-baa-baa,
Du's da best rabbit
   at ever I saa.

Da nicht is dat caald –
   du sanna geng furt.
Come here an A'll tak
   Dee up i my skurt.

Chorus: Hushie-baa, Fluffy, etc.

Da kye an da hens
   is aa ida byre
An du sall sleep here
   at da side o da fire.

Chorus.

---

starns – stars; lift – sky; trift – industry.

---

skurt – bosom (both arms enfolding).

> I kyin at du laeks
>   da aald taatit-rug
> An dere du sall lie
>   sae waarm an sae snug.

> *Chorus.*

> Sae close du dy een,
>   an faa du asleep,
> Da moarn du sall get
>   A piece o a neep!

> *Chorus.*

'Stoorbra Hill', the words of which were written by Vagaland to a tune composed by his friend Tom Georgeson, became an immediate success as a song:

> Sae golden ida golden ooers
>   da Simmer sun muvs by,
> Or baffin trowe da caavie-shooers
>   in Winter he taks wye.
> Fae Hoollan's Heichts ta Nedderdale
>   you kyin he canna will;
> An whin his time is come he sets
>   back ower fae Stoorbra Hill.

> Da folk at beelt da muckle broch
>   wis wint ta watch him tö,
> Da Udalmen aside da loch,
>   da crofters at da crö;
> An fae we baith wir young we're wrocht
>   wi wadder göd an ill,
> An traivelled, whin da hömin fell,
>   back haem fae Stoorbra Hill.

---

sae – so; ooers – hours; baffin – struggling; caavie-shooers – heavy snow showers; to will – to wander; beelt – built; broch – Pictish castle; Udalman -- one who owned his land; crö – sheep enclosure; wrocht – worked; wadder – weather; hömin – twilight.

An mony a Hairst will bring da coarn
   lang eftir we're awa,
An generations still oon-boarn
   will skyug da Winter snaa.
Dey'll watch da hedder turning green,
   da dancin simmermil,
An see da sun geng doon at nicht
   anunder Stoorbra Hill.

An see what we ir seein noo,
   da sunset's golden grinnd;
An saftly, saftly blaain trowe
   we feel da Wastern wind.
Da rodd up by da Evenin Star
   we'll kyin whaar he gengs til,
Da hidmist nicht we see da sun
   geng doon ower Stoorbra Hill.

In his introduction to *The Collected Poems of Vagaland* Ernest Marwick wrote: 'What Bredon Hill was to Housman, Stoorbra Hill was to him' (Vagaland) 'the unchanging symbol of a countryside that was indescribably dear, and of a way of life so natural and good that he coveted for future generations a perpetuation of its essential features.'

Tom Georgeson died in 1972. The song had been composed more than twenty years earlier. It was on a morning in February 1973, that I reflected how popular it had been all those years before, when it was so frequently sung by the composer himself, a splendid vocalist and musician.

An hour later, when we were booking a taxi at the British Airways office (B.E.A. as it was then), the manager mentioned in conversation that he had, the previous evening, been listening with a friend from abroad to Tom Georgeson's recording of 'Stoorbra Hill' on the Folk Society's record 'Eftir da Hömin'! This had been one of the very first recordings of Shetland songs, poetry and fiddle music, made, I think, in the early 1960s.

Down the centuries nearly all the Scots poets have been song-writers. However, a well-loved poet, William Soutar, seems to have been an exception, for Hugh MacDiarmid, when editing his poems, wrote: 'It is strange that so genuine a Scots poet as Soutar should sing so seldom.'

---

coarn – oats (in Shetland); oon-boarn – unborn; skyug – take shelter from; hedder – heather; simmermil – shimmer over sea, or quiver over hills on a hot day; grinnd – gate; blaain trowe – blowing through; rodd – road; hidmist – last.

The Shetland book of dialect songs published in 1973 contained as wide a representation as possible at that date of words and music both traditional and modern. In its initial stage of production, when it fell to me to transcribe some forty of the sixty songs, I did not visualise the form the book was to take. I mention this fact only because it gives me the opportunity to say that the venture was undertaken when my husband was already very ill, and the sense of urgency in getting the work to the printers led to errors being overlooked. It was I who read the proofs, concentrating on the dialect spelling while my husband read aloud from the manuscripts, so that all responsibility for mistakes rests with me!

It was surprising that the contributors to Radio Scotland's programme *Travelling Folk*, on 21st November 1983, when discussing Shetland music, confined their remarks to fiddle music, also a poem considered by them worthy of being set to music, but made no reference to the traditional and modern Shetland dialect songs included in the song book which my husband, in the last days of his illness, struggled so hard to complete. Two thousand copies of the book were published and sold. It is, sadly, out of print.

Some of the traditional songs have in the past been included in radio broadcasts. I recall one amusing instance where the line

Gae awaa, peerie fairies, fae wir bairn noo

in the traditional lullaby, 'Baloo-Balilli', was rendered

Gae awaa, peerie fairies, fae wir Ben Dhu!

Incidentally, I remember that this song was beautifully sung, with harp accompaniment, by Mary O'Hara some years ago in a programme of folk music broadcast from North Carolina.

I cannot claim to have any musical gifts but I grew up with a great love of Scottish songs. The battered remains of a book of *Fifty Scottish Songs* – a prized family possession for the best part of a century – survives to this day, telltale fingerprints on its pages remaining as evidence of the aspirations of would-be musicians (or songsters?) of three generations. We were not allowed to play 'by ear', and to this day I have no confidence unless there is a sheet of music in front of me. Childhood lessons were supposed to include the theory of music, but I somehow managed to conceal from both my teacher and my parents that I had no interest beyond the first page of the book of theory! My sins found me out, however, when as temporary church organist in my late fifties I decided to study music and found myself ploughing desperately through the theory grades, one by one! The knowledge acquired, however, had the 'bonus' result that I was able to assist my husband in the editing of the book of Shetland songs.

Vagaland's 'Da Sang o da Papa Men', or 'Rowin Foula Doon', the title by which it is popularly known, is included in the songbook. The melody is by Dr. T. M. Y. Manson.

> Oot bewast da Horn o Papa,
>   Rowin Foula doon!
> Ower a hidden piece o water,
>   Rowin Foula doon!
> Roond da boat da tide-lumps makkin
> Sunlicht trowe da cloods is brakkin;
> We maan geng whaar fish is takkin,
>   Rowin Foula doon!
>
> Fishy-knots wir boat haes, truly,
>   Nae misforen knot.
> We hae towes an bowes an cappies,
>   Ballast ida shott,
> Paets, fir fire ita da kyettle,
>   Taaties fir da pot.
>
> *Chorus*: Oot bewast, etc.
>
> Laek a lass at's hoidin, laachin,
>   Coortit be her vooers,
> Papa sometimes lies in Simmer
>   Veiled wi ask an shooers;
> Dan apo da wilsom water
>   Comes da scent o flooers.
>
> *Chorus*.

---

bewast – west of; tide-lumps makkin – sea piling up suddenly in a tideway; Fishy-knots – knots in boat planking said to be lucky; misforen – unlucky; towes – fishing lines; bowes – buoys; cappies – sinkers for a fishing line; shott – aftermost compartment in the bottom of a boat; ask – mist; wilsom – liable to cause one to lose one's way.

> We can bide ashore nae langer –
> We maan geng an try.
> We'll win back, boys, if we soodna
> skrime da moder-dy,
> Fir da scent o flooers in Papa
> Leds wis aa da wye.
> *Chorus.*

The tradition about the scent of flowers from the island of Papa Stour has its counterpart in the writing of John Evelyn in the seventeenth century, who says of the shrub Rosemary: 'the flowers whereof are credibly reported to give their scent above thirty leagues off at sea, upon the coasts of Spain.'

It was when visiting us one evening in the late 1960s that Dr. Manson read the newly written poem and said that it suggested a song. He there and then composed a melody for the words of the chorus, the pencilled manuscript of which I hold in its original form.

'Rowin Foula Doon' has, unfortunately, twice to my knowledge been mistakenly described as a traditional Shetland song, and, very regrettably, a plagiarised version in what I take to be Fifeshire Scots dialect, with verses containing a completely different theme, was included in a record issued by Springthyme Music in June 1983, the recording having been done by a Danish/Scots folk band calling themselves 'Kontraband'. The credits for the songs on the label of the record are shown as Robertson/Manson, for the simple reason that neither Dr. Manson nor myself, when giving permission, by phone, for the proposed inclusion of the song, had any knowledge of the alterations which had been made. Here are the words of the plagiarised version:

> Oot to sea the boats are heavin, rowin Foula doon
> Wives and bairns the men are leavin, rowin Foula doon.
> We maun gaun whaur seas are brakkin,
> We maun gaun whaur fish are takkin,
> Oot by wast the horn o Papa, rowin Foula doon.
>
> Shoot the lines and start the baitin, rowin Foula doon,
> Haul them in, nae time for waitin, rowin Foula doon.
> *(Chorus)*

---

skrime – make out; moder-dy – movement in the sea by which the haaf-men could steer their boat to land.

Catchin cod and silver whitin, rowin Foula doon
All to earn your daily livin, rowin Foula doon.
(*Chorus*)

In the sky the winds are wailin, rowin Foula doon,
Reef the main and haul the sail in, rowin Foula doon.
(*Chorus*)

All around the storm is spreadin, rowin Foula doon
Homeward now the boats are headin, rowin Foula doon.
(*Chorus*)

Boats are lost and crews are missin, rowin Foula doon,
But them that live will still go fishin, rowin Foula doon.
(*Chorus*)

This is an unfortunate travesty of the original song, for it will be seen that the optimism of the fishermen about to set out from their isle in fine weather, and confident of a safe return even if the mists should descend and obscure their island from view, has been replaced by words of 'doom and gloom'. The hazards of deep sea fishing of olden times are, of course, only too well known, and have often been the subject of Scottish song, as in 'Caller Herrin', but this was not the theme of Vagaland's poem.

Incidentally, the words 'rowin Foula doon' would apply only to the outward sea voyage, so the use of these words *ad lib* in the plagiarised version do not make sense.

Tom Georgeson, who composed music for, and sang, many Vagaland songs, had a particular gift for conveying the mood of the poetry and employing its musical rhythms. 'Yöle Day ida Yard', for instance, a celebratory poem, always seems to me to suggest an 'invitation to the dance' – a good old-time reel, perhaps? – and it was given a lively tune.

> Da hey is aa ita da dess,
>   Da coarn ita da scroo;
> A'm shöre we'll hae a fouth o maet
>   Ta set afore da coo.
>
> We're ripit aa da taaties up,
>   An gaddered every neep,
> An shön A'll hae ta seek da hill
>   An look among da sheep.

A'll try ta fin a muckle hug
Ta pit apo da pin,
Fir folk sood never want fir flesh
Whin Yöle is comin in.

We elt an varg trowe Voar an Hairst,
At times we tink it hard,
Bit we gie up aa tochts o wark
Whin Yöle comes ida yard.

The word 'elt' means to work under dirty conditions, and 'varg' also means to work under unpleasant conditions. They are apt words, indicating the hardships of crofting life. The third verse refers to the process by which mutton is 'reestit' (dried) and kept for winter use. Reestit mutton soup is still a popular winter dish.

'Da Dance o da Sooth-wast Wind', also a song, to my mind really does convey the feeling of a soft summer breeze blowing in from the sea:

Da Sooth-wast wind comes in da voe
Whaar peerie waves is laachin low,
An Simmer ask is lyin waarm
   Awa oot ower da haaf.
Apon his fit he gengs sae licht
He doesna brak da bubbles bricht
At's here an dere among da froad
   Fae shore-breach brakkin aff.

A drummie-bee is bumblin roond
An makkin sic a sleepy soond
Among da red an yallow flooers
   In whaar da blackbird biggs.
Da wind jimps ower da gairden waa
An dere he dances wi dem aa,
An dan he gengs oot ower ta see
   Da mödow an da riggs.

---

laachin – laughing; ask – mist, haze; haaf – ocean; froad – foam; shore-breach – foam and bubbles caused by breaking sea; drummie-bee – bumblebee; biggs – builds; mödow – meadow.

Night-Scented Stock in Bloom?

> Fir he's da fainly wind at laeks
> Ta kyin what happens in-a-daeks;
> He'll nedder brak da taatie-sho
>   Or ruin da growin breer.
> Da winds fae some ill-vandit erts
> Dey bring a caald ta brak folk's herts,
> Bit dey maan slip dir frosty grip,
>   Whin da Sooth-wast wind comes here.

In May 1979, the Lerwick Choral Society visited Lerwick's friendship town, Maaloy in Norway, and, according to the town's local press, provided a concert which held their audience spellbound. But the highlight of the performance appears to have been the inclusion in the programme of three songs in the Shetland dialect, the music of which was by Dr. George Ewen, himself the singer. Two of these songs were created from Vagaland poems, one of which, 'Faeroe Fishin', is included elsewhere in this book. The other, 'Starka Virna' (meaning 'bad weather'), is a quite outstanding dialect poem, which features in a tribute paid by Ernest Marwick in *The Orcadian* in 1974, shortly after Vagaland's death. After quoting this verse from 'A Skyinbow o Tammy's' (*Laeves fae Vagaland*, 1952):

> "Dat's aa geen noo" – Ya, I kyin it
>   mony a thing is geen fir aa.
> Nooadays der very little
>   o da aald wyes left ava.
> Tinks du, wid da folk be better,
>   if dey cöst da rest awa?

Ernest Marwick went on:

'It is a question which pierces perhaps to the heart of our current situation. His (Vagaland's) mind, nevertheless, was basically affirmative (the more so as he grew older), and in "Starka Virna" he voiced the hope that the native virtue of Shetland would triumph:

---

fainly – attractive, amiable; kyin – know; in-a-daeks – inside the boundary wall of a croft; taatie-sho – potato haulm; breer – first shoots of a crop; ill-vandit – (here) disagreeable.

Rain-gös,[1] rain-gös, whaar is du fleein?
– Geen is da folk at wid watch fir dee,
Fae da crofts o Vaila, da beach o Havra,
An aa da isles aroond Hildasey.
Der nae men left ida Wast isles livin
Ta draa up da boats anunder da lee,
An mak aa fast fir a boo o wadder,
Whin dey see da rain-gös gyaain ta da sea.

Rain-gös, rain-gös, whaar is du fleein?
– Ower places empty, an guidit-ill.
On mony a hert da fire is slokkit,
Bit we number twenty thoosand still,
An it's no ower late ta shange fir da better,
If onlie we hae wan mind an will –
Ta bring back life ta da deein islands –
Rain-gös, rain-gös, geng ta da hill!

'Vagaland lived to see Shetland greatly revitalised, but when hopes of its future were at their brightest the threat to the county posed by North Sea Oil came like a thunder cloud into the clearing sky. He was aware of all that could happen to the islands he loved – as I discovered when I discussed the situation with him last April – but he had been given the graces of faith and acceptance. He believed firmly that there are powers in the universe stronger than greed and materialism.'

In August 1979, I visited for the first time the 'Oil Complex' at Sullom Voe, which was expected to be completed in 1981, when it would be 'the largest in Europe'. The estimated cost at that time was, I think, said to be two billion pounds. It was little thought a few years ago that these remote islands could produce 'the largest' of anything, thus competing with the other 'wonders' of the Western world!

Whatever benefits may have come to Shetland (and some of the native population) through the oil industry, they can only be regarded as tempo-

---

[1] The rain-gös (red-throated diver) was observed to fly inland in fine weather (to nest?).

boo o wadder – continuation of the same kind of weather; guidit-ill – neglected; slokkit – extinguished; hert – hearth.

rary, and the future of her indigenous industries is largely in doubt. High wages paid by the oil industry during its development attracted labour away from areas of employment on which the islands' survival had in the past depended – principally fishing and hosiery. A generation and more has already grown up which has never known the conditions under which, formerly, a mere subsistence had to be wrested from land and sea.

Vagaland's 'Land of the Northman', translated from the Norwegian of Ivar Aasen,[2] sets the scene as it was in bygone days:

> In the midst of the rocks by the ocean
>   Has the home of the Northman been set;
> He has planned it with care and devotion
>   And has built it with toil and with sweat.
>
> He has looked at his sea-beaten border
>   That was covered with boulder and stone.
> 'Let us clear it, and set it in order;
>   And whatever we build is our own.'
>
> He has looked at the wild water breaking
>   In the lonely and dangerous sea,
> But the grey fish are his for the taking
>   And a fisherman truly is he.
>
> In the dark days he well may be thinking:
>   'I could wish for a sunnier strand.'
> But the sun o'er the hills softly blinking
>   Will rekindle his love for his land.
>
> And when hillsides are green on a June-day,
>   And the blossoms are bright on the ground,
> And the nights are as light as the noonday,
>   There is no better place to be found.

---

[2] Ivar Aasen (1813–1896) – 'linguistic genius' (according to Chambers' *Biographical Dictionary*) who initiated Landsmal or Nynorsk based on Norway's original Norse dialect. His poem '*Millom Bakkar og Berg utmed Havet*' became a song, set to a Norwegian folk melody which is now also the tune of 'Land of the Northman'.

Chapter 27

The Sound of Music

In 1970 *Da Mirrie Dancers*, a book of Shetland Fiddle Tunes edited by Tom Anderson and Tom Georgeson, was published for the Shetland Folk Society by *The Shetland Times*, Lerwick. The part played by my husband, as Secretary of the Folk Society, in the assembly of this book, with its explanatory foreword, and so on, need hardly be stressed here. Though he claimed to be 'tone-deaf', he had a remarkable appreciation of fiddle music, and from the rhythms alone could supply names to many tunes. His early poem, 'A Skyinbow o Tammy's', introduced with words from Browning, 'When you sat and played toccatas, stately at the clavichord', retains the music and rhythm of the Browning poem 'A Toccata of Galuppi's', while indulging a personal nostalgia:

> Oh, man, Tammy, dis is vexin,
> Hearin what du haes ta say;
> Boy, I tink du'll tak da fiddle –
> I wid laek ta hear dee play
> As du played at rants an haemfirs
> mony a time afore dis day.

---

haemfir – celebration after a wedding.

Night-Scented Stock in Bloom?

Yun's 'Da Mirry Boys o Greenland',
  bit da Greenland men is geen;
'Underhill',[1] fae first I heard him
  mony a heavy day A'm seen.
Whin du plays 'Aald Swaara' ta me,
  boy, da taers comes ta my een.

Minds du, whin we baith wir younger,
  foo I ösed ta sit an look
At da muckle yatlin kyettle
  hingin rampin ida crook,
An du played dy lichtsome skyinbows
  inbee at da shimly-neuk.

'Dat's aa geen noo' – Ya, I kyin it;
  mony a thing is geen fir aa.
Nooadays der very little
  o da aald wyes left ava.
Tinks du, wid da folk be better
  if dey cöst da rest awa?

Trowe wir minds wir ain aald language
  still keeps rinnin laek a tön;
Laek da laverik ida hömin,
  sheerlin whin da day is döne;
Laek da seich o wind trowe coarn
  at da risin o da mön.

---

[1] The tune 'Underhill' was first recorded from the playing of Peter Fraser of Finnigarth, Walls, and according to Folk Book, Volume One, it was at that time only known in the Walls area. 'Tammy', addressed in the poem, was an extremely gifted young fiddle player – a schoolmate of Vagaland's brother, Dody. He lost his life when his Merchant Navy ship was torpedoed in World War II.

ösed – used; yatlin – iron; rampin – boiling noisily; skyinbow – Shetland reel-tune; shimly-neuk – chimney corner; sheerlin – singing; seich – sigh.

Hit's da skriechin o da swaabie,
    an da kurrip o da craa,
An da bulder o da water
    in aboot da brakkin baa;
Hit's da dunder o da Nort wind
    whin he brings da moorin snaa.

Hit's da soond da sheep maks nyaarmin
    whin you caa dem on afore,
An da noise o hens, aa claagin,
    laying Paece-eggs ida Voar;
An da galder at da dug gies,
    whin a pik comes ta da door.

Wirds laek Freddie Stickle's music
    whin he played 'Da Trowie Burn',
Wirds wi fire an frost ita dem,
    wirds at nearly maks you murn.
Some we hae, baid coorse an haemly,
    nane can better dö da turn.

Things at maks dis life wirt livin,
    dey're jöst laek da strainin-post;
Whin he's brokken, hit's no aesy
    gettin new eens – an da cost,
Hit'll shön owergeng da honour
    if da aald true wyes is lost.

    It seems that the majority of young people in present days prefer the sound of the guitar to that of other instruments. The 'pop groups' appearing from time to time on TV are apparently limitless in number. What becomes of them all? Do their tastes in music change as they grow older, and, if so, where do their preferences then lie?
    Never before, one imagines, has the competitive spirit entered so furiously into the capacity for making sound, most of which is fortified by electronic or, no doubt, other more modern means. I remember being at a

---

skriechin – crying sound (here of birds); kurrip – croak; bulder – loud gurgling sound; brakkin ba – sea breaking on sunken rock; dunder – loud noise; moorin – drifting; owergeng da honour – be too big a price to pay.

country wedding some years ago, and being bombarded with the 'sound of music'! While trying to converse with a friend, I could not help thinking of the line spoken by Lorenzo in *The Merchant of Venice* – 'Here will we sit and let the sound of music creep in our ears'!

I find that the *Concise Oxford Dictionary* 1964 defines 'music' thus: 'Art of combining sounds of voice(s) or instrument(s) to achieve beauty of form and expression of emotion. . . . Pleasant sound, e.g. song of bird, murmur of brook, cry of hounds.'

My edition of Chambers' *Dictionary* has a more old-fashioned definition: 'A connected series of sweet sounds; melody or harmony; the art of combining sounds so as to please the ear . . .'

Not many of my 'coincidences' have been connected with music, but one which may be worth mentioning occurred in July 1975, when a sudden notion impelled me to look for a book of piano solos, in my possession but neglected for some years. After leafing through the pages to find a piece perhaps 'within my range', I decided to attempt Schumann's 'Warum?'. Later, I resumed my bedtime reading of *The Weald of Youth* by Siegfried Sassoon and found him describing how 'Wirgie', an elderly friend of the family, had frequently entertained them with her piano playing. 'Warum?' was one of the music pieces he particularly remembered!

Music defined as 'pleasant sound, e.g. song of bird' (*Concise Oxford Dictionary*) encourages the introduction here of 'Da Sang o da Blackbird' by Vagaland.

> I listened til a blackbird
>   at sang oot by my door,
> An I wis blyde ta hear him
>   dat caald, bricht day in Voar.
>
> He held nae habitation,
>   nae röf abön his head,
> Bit if he fan a gairden
>   he caredna whaar he bedd.
>
> An he wis aye bön lucky
>   ta fin enyoch ta aet;
> Sae lang as folk wis kindly
>   he didna want fir maet.

I tocht; 'Da day gets langer;
  da year's wark is begun;
An aa da Eart seems brichter
  as heicher climms da sun.

'New life trowe aa at's livin
  is rinnin laek a spring;
Da flooer maan seek da sunlicht;
  da blackbird böst ta sing.

'Bit less fir mony a boddie
  at bears a wecht o grief,
An haesna muckle comfort,
  an canna get relief.

'At times we laekly winder
  why sorrow lests sae lang
Bit we wid be da poorer
  withoot da blackbird's sang.'

Da caald wind blew nae langer;
  da sun wis by da ert.
I heard da blackbird singin
  a sang ta waarm da hert.

He sang, an never mindit
  at Winter could be drear.
Sae may da Lord aye strenten
  wir herts fae year ta year.

There was a strong element of stoicism in Vagaland's character. The song 'McPherson's Farewell' – the words are by Robert Burns – to which we both listened when it was sung on television about a month before his death, made a strong appeal to him, and has poignant memories for me. He asked me to reach down our book of Burns' poetry in which the original words appear. The last verse reads:

  Now farewell light, thou sunshine bright,
    And all beneath the sky!
  May coward shame distain his name,
    The wretch that dare not die!

Although I do not know the circumstances in which it was written, William Soutar, who, according to Hugh MacDiarmid, seldom 'sings' in his poetry, has the brave line:

>   Gang doon wi a sang, gang doon.

One of Scotland's champion fiddlers, Arthur Robertson (although of the same name, he was not related to the poet) composed a few years ago a fine slow air with the title 'Vagaland'. He had intended to name it 'Lament for Vagaland', but to me in my conviction that my husband had now reached his Tir Nan Ogh, it seemed, somehow, that we must not lament.

Chapter 28

A Scottish Dialect?

In September 1976, I was persuaded to attend as a delegate at our Church Assembly in St. Andrews, and before leaving for the south learned that I would be expected to contribute an item about Shetland to a social evening programme being arranged for delegates. As I had, in my many solitary walks, found consolation in memorising a number of my husband's poems, it was not difficult for me to decide what form my contribution should take. Indeed, I had a conviction that this was yet another occasion on which I was being guided to obtain a wider audience for these dialect poems which so far seemed not to be recognized as part of Scotland's heritage. It is somewhat paradoxical that speech in Scotland infiltrated through the centuries by English, French, Norse, and other influences, is accepted without question as the 'Scots tongue', while speech in Shetland (a part of Scotland) whose original Norn survives in Norn words and phrases but which has been deeply infiltrated through recent centuries by Scottish (and English) influences, is still virtually excluded from being part of the Scottish heritage.

In a review, in *The Scotsman* of 11th September 1965, of the book *Mair Laeves fae Vagaland*, George Campbell Hay wrote: 'It is nothing unexpected that three of the translations (from other languages), should be from the Norwegian. Yet, after all this, Shetland is Scottish, and Scots must have the breadth of mind to live with Norn as they live with Gaelic, Scots and English.'

Of course, present-day Shetland dialect, whether spoken or written, can no longer be described as 'Norn', which was the Scandinavian speech of the islanders in 1469, and probably for at least two centuries afterwards, but, as Vagaland says in 'Shetlanrie', 'Der Norn wirds atil it' (there are Norn words in it).

Night-Scented Stock in Bloom?

An *Anthology of Scottish Comic Verse*, edited by Maurice Lindsay, excludes Gaelic poetry and poetry of the Highlands and Islands, it being explained in the foreword that the anthology is mostly confined to poetry in Lowland Scots. Bearing in mind that the Shetland dialect has a strong affinity with Middle (Lowland) Scots, one feels that Vagaland's highly humorous poem 'Shetlanrie' might well have been included. Its humour, pure and refreshing, indicates the complex origins not only of the Shetland dialect but of all languages, even those regarded as 'national'.

The poem which I chose to recite at our church assembly social was called 'Vaigin On'. Not having attempted a recitation in public since I was a very small child, and then only in front of village hall audiences, I kept wondering how on earth I was going to be able to face a large audience at St. Andrews. I am not ashamed to say that in the quiet of my room, before attending the social, I prayed, on my knees, for strength and courage. This was given.

Vaigin On

Week eftir week, whin we wir young,
    an dat's a while sin syne,
We sat ita da Sunday Scöle
    wi days baith coorse an fine.

We read da stories ower an ower
    o Him at ruled da sea
An did sae mony windros things
    awa in Galilee.

We read da Bible, said wir verse,
    an sang da bairns' hymes.
– I couldna sing sae weel as some,
    bit laekit weel da rhymes.

Da things we learned ita dat scöle
    wis mair as meets da ee:
We took dem wi wis whin we göd
    ta sail oot ower Life's sea.

Scöle – School; windros – wonderful.

A Scottish Dialect?

Fir we're jöst laek da boat, ye kyin,
    at tecks across da voe:
Da sails an riggin, dey're abön,
    da ballast, hit's below.

A boat at's ballastless sails weel
    apo a Simmer sea:
Wi a göd crew alang wi you
    you dönna drive ta lee.

Hit's no sae aesy whin you hae
    ta sail a boat yoursell,
Ta keep her aff o baas an kletts
    or steer her trowe a gael.

Though some wid fling oot aald beliefs
    an mak a mockery
O faith, an wark, an everything
    – aa at da past can gie,

Da faith o single-hertit men
    da veeshon, an da draem,
Dey're ballast-stens fir ony een
    at's far an far fae haem.

An still, nae maitter if da nicht
    is mirk as he can be,
Da licht at sheened ower Bethlehem
    still sheens across da sea.

It is possible that the majority of people today are unaware that the socialist movement had its beginnings in the teachings of Christianity and that many early enthusiasts in the movement maintained their own Sunday schools, where essential principles and standards of conduct were taught. It happens that I find this entry, dated 8th October 1972, in my husband's notebook.

---

tecks – tacks; voe – sea inlet; drive ta lee – lose course; baas an kletts – sunken rocks; gael – gale; veeshon – vision; mirk – dark; sheened (Scots dialect word) – shone.

'In *The World this Weekend* it was stated that the man who was an adviser to the previous Labour government had congratulated the Conservative prime minister on his plan to introduce flat rate increases in order to solve the problem of inflation. When asked why the Labour people had not thought of this, he replied that they were concerned with "differential norms".

'How can anyone who advocated percentage increases in wages call himself a Socialist? How far does a policy of "differentials" agree with the precepts of Socialism which were taught at Socialist Sunday schools forty years ago?

In the *Concise Oxford Dictionary* 'serendipity' is described as 'the faculty of making happy and unexpected discoveries by accident', and people with experiences like mine are sometimes said to have this faculty. But the very word 'faculty' implies a competence or power, which I do not have. My own view is that extraordinary sequences of events were in some way triggered by my deep and emotional involvement in the promotion of my husband's poetry. For example:

'Yesterday (22nd April 1982) when gathering together copies of *The Reader's Digest* to take to our eventide home in Lerwick, I discovered among them a July 1975 issue of *The Scots Magazine*. Thinking that I must have kept it because it contained a review of my husband's *Collected Poems*, published in 1975, I consulted its book review pages, and, although I found my assumption to be wrong, felt a compulsion to 'stop in my tracks' and read through all the reviews, feeling the while slightly irritated because I could ill afford the time!

'But one review in particular I read twice. It began: "If the name of Francis Crawford of Lymond means nothing to you, then you have not been reading the series of historical novels by Dorothy Dunnet that have been appearing since the early sixties . . ." Now, I must confess that the name Francis Crawford of Lymond meant nothing to *me*, hardly surprising because my reading in the last decade or more has included very few novels. But the name certainly means something to me since this morning, when it was announced that next week's guest on *Desert Island Discs* – 30th April – was to be Dorothy Dunnet, "author of the series *Crawford of Lymond*"!'

A Scottish Dialect?

Even more extraordinarily, however, when listening to the interview with Dorothy Dunnet on 30th April, I learned that her husband is Alastair Dunnet, former Editor of *The Scotsman*, who, on 12th July 1956, in a letter to the then Editor of the *New Shetlander*, wrote thus about one of Vagaland's poems:

> 'I am very much interested in the two poems you sent and wonder if Vagaland will be good enough to agree to our publishing "Kwarna Farna" in *The Scotsman*. It is quite a striking piece of work. I shall keep the manuscripts by me until I hear from you.'

The poem was, in fact, 'highlighted' as a feature page of *The Scotsman* two weeks later in July 1956. It appears in this book in the chapter dealing with the origins of the Shetland dialect.

An experience, linking a television programme with my reading, occurred on 20th May 1982, when a film was shown of one of the earliest survey expeditions in the Antarctic, in the year 1912. I was greatly moved as I watched members of this expedition battling with appalling weather conditions in those far-off snowy wastes 'with gales gusting to 150 miles per hour' (to quote the account in the *Radio Times*). The disclosure that two brave men, Mertz and Ninnis, perished in this venture, added to my emotion, and I thought of our own brave task force now positioned in the South Atlantic, ready to face not only hostile weather but, in addition, the formidable hazards of war.

As I knew that Scott's expedition to the South Pole took place in 1912, I turned to my *Biographical Dictionary* to refresh my memory about that event, and read again of the gallant action of Oates. This done, I resumed my reading of Cliff Hanley's book, *The Scots*. He deals with his subject mostly in a light, humorous vein, and in the chapter which I now commenced he describes some of the fare which the hardy Scot has always enjoyed, and concludes that had Scott and Oates been well provisioned with mutton pies, their expedition might have had a different ending!

Chapter 29

Guiding Us . . .

My own enthusiasm for my husband's poetry has led me into some interesting correspondence. In June 1977, *The Aberdeen Press and Journal* contained a review by Cuthbert Graham of a book called *The Renaissance of Wonder in Children's Literature* by Marion Lochhead. The review commenced by saying how 'towards the end of last century a new kind of fairy story to delight and beguile young people began to appear in English. The pioneer of this new genre was George MacDonald from Huntly.' Cuthbert Graham went on to say that 'the same spirit that George MacDonald brought into story-telling is still being carried on by writers like George Mackay Brown, Richard Adams, Joan Aitken and several others.'

Knowing that my poet husband must rank well to the fore of the 'several other' successors of George MacDonald, whose pioneering work of introducing the element of wonder in children's literature Miss Lochhead's book now commemorated, I decided to write to her, at the same time sending a copy of *The Collected Poems of Vagaland* which had been published in 1975. In my letter I explained that I felt my husband's life and outlook had been greatly influenced by MacDonald's books, which he had read in childhood. With access to a limited selection of reading in our small village school library of seventy odd years ago, the books he read then seem to have included George MacDonald's *Malcolm* – probably his favourite – and others such as *Robert Falconer* and *Alex Forbes*, all of which remain on my bookshelves up to the present day. In more recent years he added to his collection *The Golden Key – A Study of the Fiction of George MacDonald* by Robert Lee Wolfe (Yale University Press, 1961).

On one or two occasions, when holidaying in Aberdeenshire, we paid a visit to Huntly – the last time was, I think, in 1972, only a year or so before his death. And in the school at Huntly we saw, where they were temporarily stored, some of the (handwritten) manuscripts of the novels.

There is a telling paragraph in Cuthbert Graham's review: 'George MacDonald (1824–1905) was the son of a Huntly miller. The facts of his life are strange and unusual. He graduated at King's College, entered the ministry of the Congregational Church and offended the congregation of his first charge at Arundel by preaching the love and the fatherhood of God in a measure far beyond their approval.'

In the poetry of Vagaland, who, like his illustrious forerunner, had the mind of a poet and seer, the theme of love finds constant expression.

The letter I received from Miss Lochhead thanking me for the book of poems led to further correspondence, which, with her kind permission, is reproduced here:

9th May 1980

Dear Miss Lochhead,

You may recall that I wrote to you in June 1977, after reading Cuthbert Graham's press review of your book *The Renaissance of Wonder in Children's Literature* (which I was able to purchase soon after, and read with much enjoyment). My interest at that time had been particularly aroused because you, like my husband, had such a love for the books of George MacDonald. And so I was inspired to send you a copy of *The Collected Poems of Vagaland* (T. A. Robertson).

'Now, as I feel sure you will agree, life is full of strange 'coincidences'. They have happened so frequently to me since I finished editing that book of poems that I noted them down as they occurred, and now am actually engaged in writing a book – my very first, at the age of 72! – which explains why the Shetland dialect exists, quotes at intervals my husband's poetry, comments on life as it is being lived today, and describes, as the writing proceeds, many of the extraordinary coincidences which have constantly kept me aware that we are surrounded by the thoughts of those who have loved us, but who have 'departed this life' (words which I insisted must be written on my husband's tombstone). The poem 'Night-Scented Stock', written not many months before my husband died, came to have far more meaning than I had realised when I placed it at the end of the poetry book.

I must explain, without further preamble, why I am writing to you. For a year or two I have been visiting daily a dear old neighbour, giving a little help here and there, and trying to select library books which might interest her. She had always enjoyed reading until her eyesight failed, and it was not easy to find good light reading which she had not already read, but – and this is the interesting point – the book which she was enjoying in her last illness was *The Blue Heaven Bends over All* by Jane Oliver. When I had chosen the book, I had noticed it had an introduction by you, and determined I must read it myself, which I did later.

And then I discovered a reference to another of Jane Oliver's books *Morning for Mr. Prothero*, a title which I had certainly heard before, but as I explain in my book I have never read widely until these last six years. As you will know so well, the theme of *Morning for Mr. Prothero*, though the book is written as a novel, is strangely akin to the theme of life either side of the 'border', which my 'coincidences' mean for me.

In one of my chapters I am already quoting, from Jane Oliver's book about Sir Walter Scott, *The Blue Heaven Bends over All*, the old Scots inscription she found on a tombstone: 'He yt tholis overcomis', because the relative pronoun there so strongly resembles the Shetland dialect 'at' (Da Sangs at A'll Sing ta Dee).

I should very much like to make reference to you and Jane Oliver in my book, and it would be so wonderful if you could allow me to quote from the letter you sent me when you received my husband's poems. Here is what you wrote:

27th June 1977

My dear Mrs. Robertson,

You have made not merely my day but my week (and more) bright by your kindness in writing to me, and sending that golden gift of poetry. Thank you with all my heart, and for the letter from a daughter of my beloved George MacDonald, which I shall treasure.

I look forward to many a reading of the *Poems*, but already have found delight. Indeed, the dialect is not difficult, and the glossary itself is fascinating. I enjoy words. The Selkie legends are haunting; and I love Da Peerie Folk; and the wonderful Swan's Gaet; the religious poems too: that miracle of the Easter daffodils on the altar (that is in my way of devotion); and the

Bairn-Rhymes. But it is a golden box of jewels and I shall keep looking at them continually, with profound gratitude to you, to him the poet, and to the Maker of poets.

Yours sincerely,

Marion Lochhead

I am grateful to Miss Lochhead for giving me permission to quote the above letter. In her reply she also told me about the sad circumstances of Jane Oliver's death shortly after completion of the novel[1] about Sir Walter Scott, the typescript of which she had wished Miss Lochhead to read. I could not help seeing a parallel with the circumstances of ill-health under which my husband strove to complete his last written work.

It was not until August 1983 that I copied the foregoing correspondence for inclusion with my typed MS. A few days later I noticed on a display stand in the vestibule of our local library a book by Frances Oliver and wondered momentarily whether she might be related to Jane Oliver.

However, the purpose of my visit to the library on that day was to look for a book *A Long While A-growing* by Maurice O'Sullivan, which had been recommended in the radio programme *A Good Read*. There were no books by Maurice O'Sullivan on the bookshelf but in the vacant space there was one by Jane Oliver – *In No Strange Land*! Need I say that I borrowed it for immediate reading. It had been written and published during the war years, and I discovered that although it was ostensibly a work of fiction – an imaginative reconstruction, written in the first person, of the emotional experiences of women living at selected periods of history from the first century onwards – what comes across clearly, through the words of the principal characters, is the author's personal conviction about the meaning of life, death and love. There are sentiments expressed here which need to be heard again in our own day, for example:

'It wasn't by selling other people's rights in the name of expediency that one earned the right to be free.'

'Knowledge will never glow into wisdom until love lights up its cold page.'

---

[1] *The Blue Heaven Bends over All.*

'... but when we have educated and doctored and pensioned and schemed ... still people will say: where now? And life and death and love are unpigeonholed, and they are the biggest of all.'

and regarding thought:

'Supposing that geography on the far side of the watershed depended not on the state of matter – seas and mountains and prairies – *but on the state of thought.*'[2]

'I wonder if you can ever draw the things you love most ... home too?'

Vagaland wrote of 'the thoughts of others who have truly loved us ... guiding us to a place beyond the darkness. ...'

---

[2] My italics.